Empire of Ancient Egypt

WENDY CHRISTENSEN

Facts On File, Inc.

For Alison, God's grace incarnate.

Great Empires of the Past: EMPIRE OF ANCIENT EGYPT

Copyright © 2005 Wendy Christensen

HISTORY CONSULTANT: **Dr. Josef Wegner, Associate Professor of Egyptology, University of Pennsylvania; Associate Curator, Egyptian Section, University of Pennsylvania Museum**

Facts On File, Inc.
132 West 31st Street
New York NY 10001

Library of Congress Cataloging-in-Publication Data
Christensen, Wendy.
   Empire of ancient Egypt / Wendy Christensen.
      p. cm. – (Great empires of the past)
   Includes bibliographical references and index.
   ISBN 0-8160-5558-0   (hc: alk. paper)
   1. Egypt–History–To 640 A.D.–Juvenile literature. I. Title.
II. Series.
   DT83.C49 2004
      932'–dc22   2004003951

Facts On File books are available at special discounts when purchased in bulk quantities for businesses, associations, institutions, or sales promotions. Please call our Special Sales Department in New York at (212) 967-8800 or (800) 322-8755.

You can find Facts On File on the World Wide Web at http://www.factsonfile.com

Produced by the Shoreline Publishing Group LLC
President/Editorial Director: James Buckley Jr.
Series Editor: Beth Adelman
Designed by Thomas Carling, Carling Design, Inc.
Photo research by Jullie Chung, PhotoSearch, NY
Index by Word Co.

Photo and art credits: Bildarchiv Steffens/Bridgeman Art Library: 1, 16; Giraudon/Art Resource, NY: 3, 71; Erich Lessing/Art Resource, NY: 4, 36, 55; Photography by Egyptian Expedition/The Metropolitan Museum of Art: 9, 88; Photofest: 13; Hirmer Fotoarchiv: 21; Stuart Westmorland/Corbis: 27; Facts On File, 39, 114; The Metropolitan Museum of Art, Rogers Fund and Edward S. Harkness Gift, 1929. (29.3.2): 40; Sandro Vannini/Corbis: 48; Bettmann/Corbis: 50; © The British Museum: 56, 75, 98; Vanni/Art Resource, NY: 62; Scala/Art Resource, NY: 76; Art Resource, NY: 78, 106; Louvre, Paris/France/Bridgeman Art Library: 86; AP/Worldwide Photos/Mohamad al-Shehety: 92; Josef Polleross/The Image Works: 110; Private Collection: 112; Lloyd Cluff/Corbis: 115; AP/Worldwide Photos/Mohamed El-Dakhakhny:116.

Printed in the United States of America

VB PKG 10 9 8 7 6 5 4 3 2 1

This book is printed on acid-free paper.

CONTENTS

Introduction

EGYPT, THE WORLD'S FIRST SUPERPOWER, WAS BORN ABOUT 5000 B.C.E. in the valley of the Nile River in northeastern Africa. Tucked into a long, narrow gorge threaded by the river and bounded by steep cliffs, Egypt enjoyed a predictable, mostly pleasant climate and natural barriers against invasion. To the west lay the Sahara Desert, to the east a harsh, mountainous wasteland. To the south, a series of six great rapids (called cataracts) obstructed the river. To the north was the "Great Green:" the Mediterranean Sea.

An Egyptian called his homeland *Kemet*. His world was divided into lowland *kemet* ("black land"), the narrow ribbon of rich, black earth on the valley floor, and highland *deshret* ("red land"), the pale, reddish sand of the forbidding desert plateaus. Foreigners were "highlanders." "Going up" meant leaving the valley; "descending" was returning home.

Egypt was a long, narrow oasis carved by the Nile River through the harsh desert. "The Egypt to which we sail nowadays is… the gift of the river," said Greek historian and traveler Herodotus. The Nile, one of the world's longest rivers, flows more than 4,200 miles north from central Africa to the Mediterranean. The name "Nile" comes from the Greek word Neilos, but the Egyptians called it simply *iteru*, "the river."

The Two Lands

Because all life came from the Nile, geography was everything in ancient Egypt. The narrow valley through which the Nile ran, and the wider Delta where it flowed into the sea, were known as the "two lands" of ancient Egypt. Upper Egypt, *Ta-Shomu* ("narrow land"), was a long, narrow, lime-stone gorge, 10 to 30 miles wide, stretching from the first cataract at Aswan

WHAT ARE CONNECTIONS?

Throughout this book, and all the books in the Great Empires of the Past series, you will find Connections boxes that point out ideas, inventions, art, food, customs, and more from this empire that are still part of our world today. Nations and cultures in remote history can seem far removed from our world, but these connections demonstrate how our everyday lives have been shaped by the peoples of the past.

to the edge of the Delta, 500 miles to the north. It was bounded by cliffs that rose from a few hundred feet to almost 1,000 feet high. In ancient times, Upper Egypt's floodplain totaled 42,500 square miles. Cultivated lands extended from just over one and a half miles wide at Aswan to about 13 miles wide on the west bank opposite modern Tell el-Amarna.

About 100 miles south of the Mediterranean, the Nile split into two streams and many smaller tributaries. It formed the fan-shaped Nile Delta, an 8,500-square-mile region of marsh and heavily silted land called Lower Egypt, *Ta-Mehu* ("water-filled land").

The ancient Nile had at least five, and as many as 16, outlets to the sea. (The modern Nile has only two, Rosetta and Damietta.) About 50 miles southwest of the Delta's apex lay the Faiyum. Connected underground to the Nile, the ancient Faiyum was a wetlands paradise, thick with lotus and papyrus plants and teeming with birds and animals. Birket Qaran, a lake in the northern Faiyum, was a favorite hunting spot.

The Nile (then and now) blends two major streams. The White Nile rises from the clear waters of Lakes Victoria, Albert, and Edward in central Africa. As it flows north, it gathers water from over 1,500 miles of tributaries. The Blue Nile rises in Lake Tana, in the highlands of Abyssinia (modern Ethiopia). It flows more than 1,000 miles before joining the White Nile. The two streams join at Khartoum, capital of the modern Republic of the Sudan, and flow another 1,900 miles to the sea. About 140 miles north of Khartoum, the Atbara River, rising from the Ethiopian highlands, joins the Nile.

Near Khartoum, the Nile enters a region of hard sandstone. As it runs through this difficult land, there are six lengths—the cataracts—where it has been unable to carve a clear channel. Stony outcroppings, rapids, and small but treacherous falls obstruct navigation. The northernmost cataract (the first) is closest to Egypt. Once past the first cataract, near the modern city of Aswan, sandstone gives way to softer limestone. This made it much easier for the Nile to carve a relatively straight channel. After passing the island of Elephantine, the Nile enjoys a 675-mile, unobstructed passage to the Delta and the Mediterranean Sea.

The Inundation

Each year, spring rains and melting snows in the Ethiopian highlands poured into the Blue Nile, carrying huge quantities of volcanic silt (fine particles of earth) and decaying vegetation. These "green waters," saturated with minerals and organic material, started to reach Egypt by June.

A month later, a wave of muddy water, enriched with silt and red earth, poured into the Nile from the Blue Nile and the Atbara. It washed over the valley floor, depositing millions of tons of mineral-laden silt, potash, and organic materials.

The waters continued rising until mid-September, then gradually receded. In October, the waters rose again briefly, then receded until spring. By the end of May, the Nile was at its lowest level of the year, and the land was dry and cracked.

This annual flood—called the inundation—was treasured and feared. It brought life and fertility; Egypt's civilization would have been impossible without it. But it could also bring trouble—from temporary inconvenience to major catastrophe.

When the inundation arrived on time and was neither too high nor too low, planting and harvesting went smoothly. If the inundation arrived earlier or later than usual, crop yields might be dangerously low. And a low Nile or a high Nile could spell disaster. With a low Nile, the floodwaters did not reach some of the farmlands. These lands could not be planted—there was no way to get enough water to them. A single low Nile year caused some problems, but stored grain usually came to the rescue. A series of low Niles could bring widespread famine.

In a high Nile, floodwaters swept away homes, villages, herds, dams, and canals. Thousands of people drowned or were left homeless.

The Egyptians worshiped the vital inundation as Hapi, a chubby god with a papyrus plant growing from his head. They held festivals to honor Hapi at the site of modern Gebel el-Silsila, near Elephantine, where they believed the inundation arose, and sang a hymn to Hapi: "When he appears, the land jubilates, everybody rejoices." Modern Egyptians honor this tradition by throwing flowers into the river each summer at Awru el-Nil, a national holiday that celebrates the inundation.

The Evidence of History

Ancient Egypt was one of the longest-lasting civilizations the world has ever known, spanning more than 3,000 years from about 3100 B.C.E. to 30 B.C.E.. It left an enormous amount of material for Egyptologists to study: tombs, temples, monuments, paintings, sculptures, papyrus scrolls, coffins, mummies, pottery, household goods, jewelry, clothing, toys, and more. The surviving materials are only a tiny, random fraction of what Egypt produced.

The first historian to take an interest in Egypt was Greek traveler and writer Herodotus (c.480-425 B.C.E.) who visited Egypt around 450 B.C.E.

THE NILE AS COMPASS
Upper Egypt lies south of Lower Egypt. That seems upside down. But it made perfect sense to the Egyptians because the Nile flows south to north. The Egyptian word for north meant "downstream;" their word for south meant "upstream." Most rivers flow north to south, but to Egyptians this seemed strange. Egyptian travelers were confused when foreign rivers did not behave "correctly." One Egyptian, perplexed by the Euphrates River in Mesopotamia (modern Iraq), called it "the inverted water which goes downstream in going upstream."

In Book 2 of his *Histories*, he documented places, people, and practices he saw himself. He also recorded legends and tall tales. Scholars disagree about Herodotus's reliability on many matters, especially history.

Egyptologists have found several partial lists of kings, recorded at various times during Egypt's long history. Most of these are incomplete, inaccurate, or both. Kings sometimes deliberately left out or erased the names of previous rulers, or changed inscriptions to claim previous kings' accomplishments as their own.

Egyptian Dates

It is very difficult to establish accurate dates for Egyptian history. The Egyptians did not keep a continuous timetable of years and events. Some dates can be cross-checked against records of other ancient peoples, or against known astronomical events. All dates before 664 B.C.E. are estimates.

Early dates were given relative to the years of a king's reign, or some major or unusual event ("year five of Djet," or "the second year after Djet's first expedition to Nubia"). Sometimes, dates were given relative to the national cattle census, a major event that happened every two years ("the year after Pepy's sixth counting of the oxen"). When a new king took the throne, the year was reset to one.

During the Middle Kingdom and later, dates were given only relative to each king's reign ("the 12th year of Thutmose"). Often, several kings had the same name, making dates even more complicated.

There is still much controversy among Egyptologists about dates. As new information has come to light, Egyptologists have revised Egyptian chronology several times. In the New Kingdom, dates from different sources can vary by as much as 20 years. For the Old and Middle Kingdoms, dates might differ as much as 50 years in either direction.

The dates in this book are from "Three Kingdoms and 34 Dynasties," by Dr. William J. Murnane, in David Silverman's book *Ancient Egypt*.

The king list considered most complete (although it has many mistakes) was written in Greek by the Egyptian high priest and scribe Manetho. His list extends from 3100 B.C.E. (the time of the unification of Upper and Lower Egypt) to 332 B.C.E. (when Egypt was conquered by Alexander the Great), dividing the kings into 31 dynasties (hereditary ruling families). This was the first time the rulers had been listed in this standardized way.

Manetho lived during the Ptolemaic Period, which puts him a thousand years further away in time from the earliest dynasties than we are today from his time. Neither Manetho's *Histories* nor his sources have survived. Short passages from his work, including his list of kings, were later quoted by the Roman historians Africanus, Josephus, and Eusebius, preserving them for subsequent study.

Modern Egyptologists recognize 34 dynasties: the 31 listed by Manetho, two additional dynasties for the Macedonian and Ptolemaic kings, and what they call Dynasty 0, to account for a few very early

Carter Wraps Up His Treasures
On November 4, 1922, British Egyptologist Howard Carter (1873–1939) uncovered a flight of steps leading down into the tomb of a minor Eighteenth Dynasty king, Tutankhamun. Carter removed a few stones from the door that sealed the tomb and peered into the chamber. "Can you see anything?" asked Earl of Carnarvon (1866–1923), the expedition's financial backer, whom Carter had summoned from London. "Yes," Carter replied, "wonderful things." (As quoted in "The Tomb of Tutankhamen" by Howard Carter.)

kings. Egyptian kings are often called *pharaohs*, but that term was not used for the king until quite late in Egyptian history.

Because Egyptian history is so long, Egyptologists group the dynasties into periods, based on political, social, economic, and other factors they had in common. These divisions are modern inventions.

A Whirlwind Tour of Egyptian History

The 1,850 years of Egypt's Predynastic era (5000 B.C.E.–3150 B.C.E.) were busy times of intense cultural and agricultural development, population growth, widespread settlement, and the adoption of hieroglyphic writing. Egypt's population was about 1 million by the time King Narmer united the "two lands" in 3100 B.C.E.

The 375 years of the Early Dynastic Period (3000 B.C.E.–2625 B.C.E.) saw the unification of Upper and Lower Egypt under strong central rule. During Dynasties 0 to 3 the capital city of Memphis was founded, and Egypt's huge, bureaucratic government rapidly developed.

The Old Kingdom (2625 B.C.E.–2130 B.C.E.) was the age of the great pyramids. In statues of themselves, Old Kingdom rulers have a calm, god-like peacefulness. They knew they were assured of eternal life. They probably did not care much about everyday, earthly matters or the troubles of the peasants. They are portrayed speaking directly to the gods and thinking lofty thoughts. They did not hesitate to pour all Egypt's resources into building lavish tombs for themselves.

By the end of the Old Kingdom, Egypt's population had grown to 2 million, mostly extremely poor peasants. There was general unhappiness with increasingly expensive royal building projects. Powerful, wealthy local rulers started ignoring the king, and splintered Egypt into independent feudal provinces.

Climate changes brought a disastrous series of low Niles, causing crop failures, widespread famine, and the miseries of the First Intermediate Period (2130 B.C.E.–1980 B.C.E.). For 150 years, Egypt suffered chaos, civil war, and famine.

The Middle Kingdom (1980 B.C.E.–1630 B.C.E.) was a glorious but restrained era of reform and cultural restoration. In statues of themselves, Middle Kingdom rulers have the worried, care-worn expressions of men facing many real-world problems. They were wealthy and powerful, but also hard workers, running a huge, unwieldy government. They saw what chaos and civil war can do to their country. They did not want a repeat. For 350 years, Egypt enjoyed peace, prosperity, increased trade, and great practical achievements. The population grew to about 2.5 million. For the first time, Egypt had a middle class.

The Second Intermediate Period (1630 B.C.E.–1539 B.C.E.) brought Egypt's worst nightmare: rule by foreigners. Another period of climate change and unstable Nile years brought crop failure, famine, and civil disorder. The Hyksos ("rulers of foreign lands"), foreigners of Semitic origin, took advantage and seized the throne, holding it for more than 100 years. Because they were foreigners, the Hyksos were hated. But they brought much-needed fresh ideas and cultural innovations to Egypt. After a long, difficult power struggle, a group of princes from the city of Thebes drove the Hyksos from Egypt.

The New Kingdom (1539 B.C.E.–1075 B.C.E.) was Egypt's imperial age. At its greatest extent, Egypt's empire stretched from the fourth cataract of the Nile deep in Nubia all the way to the Euphrates River in Asia. Egypt was powerful and wealthy beyond compare–the world's first superpower. The imperial pharaohs of the New Kingdom have proud, confident faces. They owned the world. They thought extreme-ly highly of Egypt, and even more highly of themselves. No boast was too grand, no monument too large, no conquest too challenging for these mighty pharaohs. For more than 450 years, Egypt, now home to about 3 million people, was on top of the world. Gold, gifts, plunder, and tribute flowed in like the Nile floods. But winds of change were blowing.

During the 419 years of the Third Intermediate Period (1075 B.C.E.–664 B.C.E.) Egypt's power weakened and, eventually, the empire came to an end. By around 1000 B.C.E., Egypt was just about bankrupt.

CONNECTIONS >>>>>>>>>>>>>>>>>>>>>>>>>>>>>>>>

Popular Obelisks

Obelisks are four-sided tall, slender pillars covered with hieroglyphic inscriptions and tapering to a point at the top, usually carved from a single block of stone. They were created by the Egyptians to symbolize contact between humans on earth and the gods in the heavens. A pair of obelisks bearing commemorative inscriptions often stood at the entrance to temples, particularly those dedicated to the sun god, Ra. Their purpose was to proclaim the king's power and successes.

These obelisks captured the imagination of foreign conquerors throughout history, and many can now be found in different parts of the world. Two great obelisks, which stood in Egypt for 2,500 years, were brought to Rome to commemorate Julius Caesar. These became known as Cleopatra's Needles. Ironically, in 1878 one was transported to London and placed on the Thames River embankment. New York City received the other one, and placed it in Central Park in 1881.

Several obelisks were brought to ancient Rome in imperial times, and others were made by the Romans, who imitated Egyptian hieroglyphics to simulate the real thing. They were erected outside temples or mausoleums or along the center line of arenas built for chariot racing. When the Roman Empire came to an end, one by one the obelisks fell and were buried. It was not until the Renaissance that a renewed interest for antiquities caused them to be unearthed.

Possibly the best known obelisk in Egypt is at the Temple of Luxor in Thebe, which was raised by Ramses II. This obelisk was originally one of a pair, each 72 feet tall and 254 tons of solid red granite. In 1836, Napoleon removed one and it now stands in the Place de la Concorde in Paris.

One modern obelisk that may be familiar is the Washington Monument in the United States capital. Built to honor the first president of the United States, George Washington (1732–1799), this 555-foot obelisk is the tallest building in Washington, D.C.

The country splintered into numerous small kingdoms and fiefdoms, constantly at war. Massive confusion reigned, enabling Egypt's former colony, Nubia, to seize the throne, which it held for more than 100 years.

During Egypt's Late Period (664 B.C.E.–332 B.C.E.) outside influences and invaders–Assyrians, Babylonians, Persians, and Macedonian Greeks–dominated Egypt. A dynasty of merchant-kings, the Saites, fell to the Persian Cambyses in 525 B.C.E. The First Persian Occupation (525 B.C.E.–405 B.C.E.) was an unhappy time. Egypt did not like being part of someone else's empire. The Egyptians rebelled and won back their independence for 66 years. Nakhthoreb (also known as Nectanebo II), the last king of the Thirtieth Dynasty, who ruled from 362 B.C.E. to 343 B.C.E., was the last native Egyptian to rule Egypt for 2,300 years, until 1952.

The Second Persian Occupation (343 B.C.E.–332 B.C.E.) was brief and troubled. Egypt longed for a savior. In 332 B.C.E., Alexander the Great drove the hated Persians from Egypt, beginning the Hellenistic (Greek) Period (332 B.C.E.–323 B.C.E.). The Egyptians considered Alexander a god– the son of their god Amun-Re. In founding the city of Alexandria, Alexander brought Egypt into the greater Mediterranean world. But Egypt's ancient, native civilization was swiftly passing away.

The Ptolemaic Period (323 B.C.E.–30 B.C.E.) saw the end of ancient Egypt. The Ptolemies, ruling from Alexandria, were greatly influenced by the Greeks, and Greek and Egyptian culture began to blend. In 30 B.C.E., Queen Cleopatra VII committed suicide rather than face defeat by the Romans, and Egypt became a province of the Roman Empire.

Why Learn About Ancient Egypt?

Ancient Egypt did not leave what scholars call a successor community– an identifiable group of people who carry on some or all of the practices, beliefs, traditions, and customs of an earlier people or culture with a reasonable degree of continuity. To be a true successor community to a culture or civilization, the new culture must uphold beliefs and traditions that were integral to the original culture, and that are identifiable and distinctive.

But once Egypt became part of the Roman Empire, her religion gradually vanished. Hieroglyphic writing was abandoned, and the secret to deciphering it was lost for thousands of years. Her spoken language metamorphosed into Coptic. Her artistic styles were not adopted by other cultures. Her imperial age lasted only a few hundred years, and left little mark on a rapidly-changing world. Of all Egypt's achievements, only the 365-day calendar, adopted by the Romans, remained.

For thousands of years, ancient Egypt lay buried in sand and obscurity. But she was only sleeping. In 1798, French general Napoleon Bonaparte shook her awake with a landmark expedition to Egypt. Napoleon brought scientists, historians, artists, and scholars to explore and document the ancient monuments and ruins. In 1802, the first edition (of more than 40) of *Travels in Upper and Lower Egypt* by French artist Vivant Denon (1747-1825) caused a huge sensation in Europe. The resulting fascination produced waves of what came to be known as Egyptomania—a trend that shows no signs of slowing 200 years later. Egyptian styles of design and ornamentation have long influenced architecture, fashion, make-up, hairstyles, home décor, graphic arts, jewelry and more.

In 1809, the first edition of Denon's 36 illustrated volumes of *Description de l'Egypte* (Description of Egypt) caused another wave of

The Mummy's Curse
The 1943 movie The Mummy's Ghost *was one in a popular series of movies showing ancient mummies that came back to life. This one stars Lon Chaney as the mummy and Frank Reicher as Professor Norman.*

Egyptomania

The hippies of the 1960s adopted the *ankh*, an Egyptian symbol for eternal life, as a symbol of their movement. A new wave of Egyptomania swelled in the 1970s when objects from Tutankhamun's tomb toured world museums. Millions of visitors waited for hours to see the solid gold coffins, jewelry, and other treasures.

Recent reexamination of a mummy found in a tomb in 1898 has led some Egyptologists to suggest it may be the famous beauty Nefertiti. This startling announcement, along with a Discovery Channel special about the queen, has already set off a new wave of Egyptomania.

Many computer games use Egyptian motifs and themes. Mail-order catalogs sell CD cabinets and wine closets shaped like Tutankhamun's coffin. You can buy lamps in the form of the goddess Isis, pedestals and end tables shaped like temple columns, jewelry boxes decorated with copies of tomb-wall paintings, and figurines of the Egyptian deities Bastet, Sekhmet, Isis, Osiris, and Anubis. Scarabs and Egyptian cats are popular jewelry items. You can visit web sites that translate your name (or any text) into hieroglyphics, and buy rings and pendants with your name, in hieroglyphics, in a royal cartouche.

Egyptomania. Denon's books gave European scholars their first close look at images of Egyptian objects and inscriptions, and helped speed up the process of decoding the hieroglyphics. They also alerted potential looters. Egyptian tourism skyrocketed.

Another huge wave of Egyptomania erupted after the discovery of the tomb of Tutankhamun (popularly known as King Tut) in 1922. Egyptian design, with its elegant, angular lines and geometrical forms based on idealized plants and flowers, had a tremendous influence on the art movement of the time known as Art Deco.

Hollywood quickly picked up on the popular myth of a "curse" on King Tut's tomb. An endless series of "curse of the mummy" movies followed. Epic films "documented" the building of the pyramids and the life of Cleopatra, taking extreme liberties with the facts.

Egypt becomes more fascinating with each passing year, each new archaeological discovery, each television special, each old mystery solved, each new mystery that emerges. In many ways, the modern world is Egypt's long-delayed "successor community." We do not worship Egyptian gods and goddesses or write in hieroglyphics. But no other ancient civilization holds such intense fascination for us.

PART I

HISTORY

Egypt Before the Empire

Imperial Egypt

Egypt's Long Decline

CHAPTER 1

Egypt Before the Empire

IN EARLY PREHISTORIC TIMES, THE NILE VALLEY WAS NOT A great place to live. Each summer, floodwaters filled the narrow gorge cliff to cliff. When they receded, the valley remained wet and marshy.

But it was a hunter's paradise. The Nile was alive with fish. Papyrus thickets teemed with game birds. Antelopes, gazelles, oryxes, and wild bulls grazed in lush greenery near the cliffs. Crocodiles and hippos patrolled river shallows and muddy pools.

From 8000 to 5000 B.C.E., the Nile valley and surrounding deserts were much cooler and wetter than they are today. But the climate was changing rapidly, turning hotter and drier. The valley started drying out more quickly after the annual floods. Soon, some spots on the sandy plateaus that rose up to the cliffs were dry year-round.

Around 5000 B.C.E., people started living year-round in the Nile River valley. Great droughts in Asia had set masses of people adrift. These unwilling wanderers longed to resume the lifestyles they had left: agriculture (growing grains and other foodstuffs) and animal husbandry (tending herds of animals for meat, milk, hides, wool, and transportation). To them, the Nile valley looked very inviting.

Archaeologists have identified several Predynastic Egyptian cultures, named for modern towns where remains of ancient cultures were found. The Badarian culture arose about 5000 B.C.E. It was succeeded by the Amratian culture (also called Naqada I) about 4000 B.C.E. The Early and Late Gerzean Periods (also called Naqada II) followed around 3500 B.C.E. and 3300 B.C.E.

Because these cultures did not leave written records, it can seem that Egyptian civilization sprang out of nowhere. But it was just that the

OPPOSITE
Still a Wonder
The pyramids at the Giza Plateau still have the power to awe us, more than 4,500 years after they were built.

17

ancient Egyptians had settled down and prospered in the Nile valley long before they learned to write. Archaeologists have uncovered enough physical evidence to piece together a general picture of early civilization in the valley. But over thousands of years, the Nile's annual flood buried most evidence of Predynastic Egyptian life. What is known about these people comes mostly from cemeteries, pottery, tools, weapons, jewelry, and other metal objects.

Early Nile valley settlers carefully buried their dead in locations safe from the floodwaters. Archaeologists have discovered many cemeteries on high ground near the cliffs. Villages were located on "turtle-backs" (small rises of land) on the valley floor. Evidence of only a few valley floor settlements has survived, mostly by chance. By studying layers of mud, archaeologists and geologists have determined that many more settlements are buried deep beneath millennia of mud.

In the Delta, the Nile has gradually shifted eastward over thousands of years, wiping out signs of many important early settlements. Other ancient villages lie buried deep beneath modern towns and cities. Many of these sites have been continuously inhabited for up to 8,000 years.

Many ancient settlements were dismantled, brick by brick, by the Egyptians themselves. Most ancient buildings were made of sun-dried mud-brick. As mud-brick decays, it turns into *sebakh*—the organic debris of human occupation; it makes a cheap, handy compost and fertilizer. Over the centuries, *sebakh* gatherers have removed all traces of entire ancient villages and towns.

Predynastic Egyptians lived in small, self-supporting villages on humps of dry land near the river's edge, close to hunting and fishing grounds and to cultivated fields. They tended herds of animals. They wove baskets and mats from papyrus and reeds. They grew wheat and barley, storing the grains in pits lined with reed mats. They used milling and grinding stones and simple cooking equipment.

They protected their eyes from the harsh sun with "eye paint": minerals mixed with oils and ground on stone palettes. They pressed cleansing oils from the wild castor plant. Compared to people in other parts of the ancient world, they enjoyed a good life. Food, both cultivated and wild, was usually plentiful.

They believed in an afterlife. They laid a dead person on his left side, knees touching his chin, wrapped him in a reed mat or animal skin, or placed him in a basket, and buried him in a shallow oval pit in the sand, facing west. Graves often included jars of beer and food, pottery, make-up palettes, weapons, personal ornaments, and small figurines symbolizing fertility or life. In the hot, dry sand, bodies dried out before they had a chance to rot, creating natural mummies.

Predynastic religion included animal cults. Animal cemeteries, located near human graves, included the bodies of dogs, jackals, sheep, and cows, wrapped in linen or matting and carefully buried.

Coming Together

During the Badarian era, perhaps about 100,000 people lived in what was to be Egypt. This increased to 250,000 people during the Amratian Period. With more people to feed, better organization was necessary. Egypt always faced the danger of a low or high Nile (see page 7). When disaster struck, it took discipline, cooperation, and strong leadership to quickly restore food production and distribution.

Villages gradually banded together into confederations under strong chieftains. These regional alliances became the permanent administrative districts of dynastic Egypt. Egyptologists call these districts *nomes*, and their leaders, *nomarchs*.

During the late Gerzean era, important people such as nomarchs were buried in increasingly large, complex, rectangular mud-brick structures. Ordinary people were still buried in simple pits in the sand.

There is controversy among Egyptologists about what this two-tier burial system means. Sir Flinders Petrie (1852–1942), father of scientific archaeology, thought it meant that a "dynastic race" had invaded Egypt from the Near East or Nubia, taken over, and introduced writing and other cultural advances. Other scholars believe the social divisions were a natural part of cultural trends already in motion.

The later Gerzean Period saw increased political activity. The population continued to grow rapidly. Since there are no written records, little is known about how the nomes finally joined up, forming two distinct cultures in Upper Egypt and Lower Egypt: the Delta culture and the Naqada culture. By 3400 B.C.E. Egypt ended up with two kingdoms.

The Ta-Mehu culture in Lower Egypt's Delta had its capital at Pe (later Buto). Its king wore a red crown (known as *deshret*). Its patroness was the cobra goddess Edjo (Wadjet) and its symbols were the papyrus and the bee. While there is no evidence that the ancient Egyptians called this the Red Land, modern scholars have referred to it that way.

The Ta-Shomu culture in the long, narrow gorge of Upper Egypt had its capital at Nekhen (later Hierkonpolis). Its king wore a tall,

WHY TWO NAMES?

Sometimes you will see two names used to refer to the same god, goddess or noble person—such as the cobra goddess Edjo (Wadjet). Because Egyptian writing did not use vowels, we do not know how they pronounced their words and guesses have to be made. Thus, many ancient Egyptian words or names have three or more forms (including at least one Greek form) that are more or less accepted. For example, Thutmose is also called Tuthmosis; Taweret is also Tueris; Sesostris is also Senwosret; Khufu is also Cheops; Khafre is also Chephren—and there are many more.

conical white crown (known as *hedjet*). Its patroness was the vulture goddess Nekhbet and its symbols were the lotus and the sedge (a kind of marsh grass). This culture has come to be known as the White Land.

There were struggles for dominance among factions within each of the two lands, and between Ta-Mehu and Ta-Shomu. An ambitious local chieftain arose in Ta-Shomu, and united its districts under his rule. He then did the same in Ta-Mehu.

To piece together the story of Egypt's unification, archaeologists have made many guesses based on a small number of objects: large commemorative palettes (shield-shaped stones) and ceremonial mace heads (hammer-like weapons) carved with scenes depicting political events.

The chieftain who united the two lands (in about 3100 to 3150 B.C.E.) is traditionally called Narmer. His triumphs are depicted on the Palette of Narmer, now in the Cairo Museum. On one side, Narmer wears the white crown as he slays his foes; on the other side he wears the red crown. After Narmer, Egyptian kings wore the combined double crown (known as *sekhemty*), and adopted names and titles that symbolized their dominion over the two lands.

No one knows who taught the inhabitants of the Nile valley to write. It might have been refugees from Mesopotamia. Mesopotamian cuneiform (wedge-shaped) writing, scratched into slabs of damp clay, bears little relation to Egyptian writing. But the idea of expressing ideas using symbols could have planted a seed. Hieroglyphics, Egyptian picture-writing, emerged during the late Predynatsic Period, and hieroglyphs are found in a tomb that has been dated to 3250 B.C.E.

The Early Dynastic Period

Narmer's triumph did not put an immediate end to conflict. There were many periods of localized warfare. Forces from the north and south clashed. For awhile, the two lands continued to think of themselves as separate kingdoms.

Narmer, who was from Ta-Shomu, may have married a Ta-Mehu princess to establish his right to rule the north. Throughout Egyptian history, many kings chose wives to strengthen their ties to the royal family or to cement a political or diplomatic relationship. Second Dynasty king Khasekhemwy also married a northern princess.

This period, known as the Early Dynastic Period, covers 375 years of what Egyptologists have named Dynasties 0 to 3 (3000 B.C.E.–2625 B.C.E.). Most information about the Early Dynastic Period comes from royal tombs at Abydos, and tombs of nobles at Saqqara. The few items missed by tomb robbers show that arts and crafts were already highly advanced.

Early kings wanted to be assured of plenty of help and companionship in the afterlife. When they died, servants and family members were killed and buried with them. First Dynasty king Djer was buried with more than 300 people. This cruel, wasteful practice was abandoned by the end of the First Dynasty.

The population was growing rapidly, reaching an estimated 1 million by the end of the Second Dynasty. One of the king's most important roles was to increase food production by extending irrigation systems and reclaiming land for farming. Land was reclaimed for farms, towns, and cities using dams and drainage canals. First Dynasty king Hor-Aha founded the capital city of Memphis on land reclaimed from the Nile. Memphis (which means "white walls"), at the southern tip of the Nile Delta, became one of the ancient world's greatest cities.

Artistic, cultural, religious, and political traditions were established during the Early Dynastic Period that persisted throughout Egypt's history. At Memphis, a highly centralized, bureaucratic government was soon in

Writing on the Wall
Hieroglyphics emerged during the late Predynastic Period, and became both a sophisticated writing system and an elegant art form. On monuments they were often combined with relief carvings, as on this obelisk at Amun's Temple in Karnak. It shows the king being confirmed by Amun.

place and growing fast. The government employed legions of scribes, tax collectors, accountants, engineers, and architects. Specialists oversaw trade, irrigation, and drainage, and the distribution and storage of food.

Scribes, whose job was to write down all important records, quickly converted from cumbersome hieroglyphics, based on pictures, to speedier hieratic script (a kind of hieroglyphic shorthand). They wrote on sheets or rolls of papyrus, made from the fiber of the papyrus plant, which was already in wide use by Narmer's time. Accountants and engineers had all the basic mathematical and surveying skills they needed to determine property boundaries and calculate crop yields. The 365-day calendar was in place. A system of weights and measures simplified trade and tax collection.

Artists and craftsmen started using standardized proportion grids for depicting objects and people. Before beginning to paint or carve, the artist drew a grid of horizontal and vertical lines of predetermined size and spacing on his work surface (a tomb wall, for example). Depending upon the rank and social position of the person being depicted, he or she was made a specific size in relation to the other figures in the composition. Also, each figure had to be structured in a specific way—a person was a certain number of "heads" tall, the legs were a certain length in relation to the torso, and so on. These very specific relationships were established early on and artisans seldom deviated from them. These conventions and proportions had deep religious, magical, cultural, and social significance. (There is more information about artistic conventions in chapter 6.)

The arts of pottery and stonework were highly advanced. There is evidence of roof beams, joists, and large doors made of cedar wood, indicating ongoing trade with Lebanon, which is on the Mediterranean coast more than 200 miles northeast of Egypt. Articles of ebony and ivory show that trade with Nubia, in north-central Africa south of Egypt, was well-established. Trade goods that came through the southerly routes from Nubia originated in Nubia itself, and from the peoples of the Sudan and of equatorial and sub-Saharan Africa. Lapis lazuli ornaments show that Egyptian traders were also benefitting from a long-distance trade network that brought in gemstones and other luxury goods from as far as central Asia. The stage was set for a spectacular flowering of culture.

Early Third Dynasty kings faced serious internal political problems and could not yet afford to concentrate on tomb-building. They granted large estates, herds, and rich gifts to trusted nobles who promised to keep the provinces quiet. These nobles enjoyed enormous local power and prestige, setting up a dangerous pattern repeated throughout the dynastic era: powerful local nobles becoming too wealthy and independent.

Besides putting down internal squabbles, kings were also busy obtaining reliable supplies of the industrial materials they needed and the luxury goods they craved. Third Dynasty kings began extensive mining in the Sinai Peninsula, especially for copper and turquoise. Keeping the mines open often meant military action against local Bedouin tribes.

Keeping prized gold flowing north from Nubian mines was a problem faced by kings throughout the dynastic era. Third Dynasty king Djoser extended the boundary of Upper Egypt to the first cataract at Aswan to help secure the southern trade routes.

Djoser's success at managing internal affairs let him turn attention to his tomb. He wanted to do something different, and had just the man to do it: his brilliant vizier (chief official), Imhotep. Imhotep designed the world's first pyramid, the Step Pyramid, at Saqqara. The Step Pyramid is a stack of successively smaller mastabas (the Arabic word for "bench"; it is a small, oblong tomb with sloping sides and a flat roof) piled atop one another. It measures 467 feet by 393 feet, and is 200 feet tall. It was the first all-stone building in the world.

The Old Kingdom

The Old Kingdom spans Dynasties 4 through 8, a period of 495 years from 2625 B.C.E. to 2130 B.C.E. It was the age of the great pyramids. The rule of the god-king was absolute. He alone was privileged to enjoy eternal life. As chief priest, he controlled the Nile and the inundation, and made sure the sun rose every day. As leader of an increasingly prosperous country, he commanded enormous power and wealth. Old Kingdom kings poured all of Egypt's resources into ensuring that their afterlives would be as luxurious and glorious as possible.

For a few hundred years at the height of the Old Kingdom, all Egypt's wealth—stone, gold, and gems, every peasant's labor, every artisan's skill, the central government, and the entire religious establishment—were harnessed for a single goal: building royal tombs. Advances in architecture, astronomy, surveying, construction, quarrying, stonework, sculpture, art, and hieroglyphic writing were focused on designing, building, decorating, and maintaining the king's tomb and vast necropolis—a city of the dead, where tombs were laid out like a well-planned town.

Like Djoser, later kings also wanted pyramids. And now they had the wealth to build on a large scale. They tried several designs. During his 40-year reign, Fourth Dynasty king Sneferu built at least two pyramids of different designs: his Bent pyramid, and the Red Pyramid, both at Dahshur. The Bent pyramid was an attempt to build a true, smooth-sided pyramid. But during construction, it almost collapsed. So the builders had to reduce its almost 54-degree angle of incline to 43 degrees halfway up, resulting in a curiously asymmetrical profile. The Red Pyramid is a smooth-sided (not stepped) structure, making it the first true pyramid. Unlike the Great Pyramid and others in the Giza Plateau, the Red Pyramid at Dahshur rises at a 43-degree angle of incline.

Sneferu's son, Khufu, was the biggest builder of all. He spent his entire 25-year reign getting ready for his afterlife. It still holds many mysteries. The Great Pyramid of Khufu, second king of the Fourth Dynasty, is the only one of the seven wonders of the ancient world still standing. Khufu took the art and science of pyramid building to heights it had never achieved before, and never would again.

Khufu built his pyramid and necropolis at the edge of the desert on the northwestern corner of the Giza Plateau, southwest of modern Cairo. No one had built there before. When fully developed, the complex stretched over four miles long. It included the Great Pyramid (surrounded by an eight-foot high wall) and a huge mortuary temple for the king's funeral. A 2,700-foot-long paved causeway led to the Valley Temple by the Nile. At least five pits held boats in which Khufu's spirit could sail the heavens.

The vast necropolis included hundreds of mastabas for royals, nobles, priests, and officials. Villages housed construction workers and priests to tend to the king's cult after his death. There were three small pyramids for Khufu's queens, and a small cult pyramid—a very small pyramid used in religious/magical rituals and ceremonies during the king's funeral, and afterward as a site of rituals for his mortuary cult. It may have been meant for the king to use in some (unknown) way during his afterlife. It was excavated only recently, and its precise meaning and use within the necropolis is still a hot topic of debate among Egyptologists.

Khuit Khufu—Khufu's Horizon, as the Egyptians called the Great Pyramid—was the largest, most complex, and best built of all the pyramids. When first built, it rose 481 feet into the desert sky. (The top 31 feet, including the capstone, are long gone.) The pyramid's base covers about 13 acres. Each of the four sides is 755 feet long at the base. Until 1889, when the 1,045-foot Eiffel Tower was built in Paris, it was the tallest artificial structure on earth. It held this record for more than 4,000 years.

NOTHING LASTS FOREVER

The idea behind building a village for the living around a necropolis was that priests would tend to the king's necropolis eternally, performing rituals, providing nourishment and offerings to the dead king and his favorites buried nearby, forever. Egyptians called their tombs "houses of a milion years." In practice, however, the mortuary cults of even the grandest kings were eventualy abandoned. The tombs were plundered and stripped for building stone by tomb robbers—and later kings.

More than 2 million limestone blocks, weighing an average of two-and-one-half tons each (some weigh up to 15 tons), were stacked, with amazing accuracy, in 210 ascending rows. The blocks in the lowest row are five feet tall; the blocks at the summit are 21 inches tall. The outer walls are slightly concave (bowed inward) to increase stability. The Pyramid was topped with a gold-covered pyramidion (pyramid-shaped capstone).

No one is sure exactly how the Great Pyramid was built or how long it took. Egyptian priests told Herodotus it had taken 20 years. He calculated that the project would have required more than 100,000 workers. Modern Egyptologists believe it was more like 15,000. The pyramid builders had mostly stone-age tools. But they also had unlimited manpower, religious motivation, excellent organization, strong leadership, and plenty of time.

For measuring, the builders used ropes and sticks, a plumb bob (a weight at the end of a string), leveling staffs, and a set-square to mark angles. For cutting limestone, they used flint knives, copper chisels, long copper saws, and wooden wedges. A stonecutter, recognizing natural seams in the rock, pounded in wooden wedges, soaked the wedges, and waited for the heat of the sun to expand the wood. The wood split the rock at the seams. Harder stone was pounded free with diorite slabs, using pumice or quartz sand as an abrasive.

Most of the blocks were quarried from limestone outcrops near the site. The outer casing was fine white limestone from Tura, east of the Nile. (Most of the casing blocks are long gone, used to build medieval Cairo.) The pink granite for the burial chamber and sarcophagus (the outer stone coffin) was floated on barges from quarries near Elephantine.

At the time the Great Pyramid was built, the Egyptians had donkeys and oxen, but no horses. They did not use pulleys or wheels. The massive blocks were probably raised using earth and mud-brick ramps. The design of the ramps is a subject of much controversy. On flat ground and slight inclines, the blocks were dragged with heavy flax ropes over oiled rollers made of wood or stone.

The Great Pyramid was not built by slaves. Manual laborers, drafted from all over Egypt, worked under a core of architects, engineers, master builders, stonemasons, artisans, and scribes. Draftees were mostly farmers who had nothing to do while their fields were underwater as a result of the inundation. They worked for a season, then returned home.

The Pyramid's interior is a complex maze of chambers, tunnels, shafts, and corridors. There is much controversy about the purpose and nature of some of these features, and whether there might be still-undiscovered features inside, or beneath, the Great Pyramid.

Khufu's son, Khafre, built his slightly smaller pyramid complex near his father's. He added a unique touch: the Great Sphinx. A reclining lion with a human head and Khafre's face, this guardian of the necropolis, carved from a natural outcrop of limestone, is 60 feet tall and 240 feet long.

King Menkaure's pyramid, the third at Giza, is only half the height of the Great Pyramid. In fact, the huge pyramids of Sneferu, Khufu, and Khafre were a departure from the normal scale of the vast majority of pyramids. Many scholars think that after Khafre the emphasis turned to temples and their decoration.

As they observed the sun and the other objects in the sky, the astronomer-priests of the popular sun god Re at Heliopolis made many discoveries. They documented the movements of celestial bodies, and learned to calculate the passage of time based on the rising and setting of stars and constellations. They understood the geometry of angles and were skilled at surveying land. They guarded their scientific knowledge closely. Because its priests possessed so much useful knowledge, the solar cult became wealthy and powerful. The first kings of the Fifth Dynasty finally realized that building lavish tombs for themselves while ignoring the rest of the country was not wise. They quickly saw the advantages of being associated with Re's powerful cult. Fifth Dynasty king Userkaf built the first temple to the sun god. His successors built many more.

Fifth Dynasty pyramids were not as well built at their Fourth Dynasty predecessors: They were constructed with rubble or mud-brick cores covered with stone casings. When the outer stone was stolen for other buildings (as always happened, sooner or later), the pyramids crumbled. Since the pyramids could not be relied on to stand forever, kings started looking to magic to ensure a comfortable afterlife. The tomb of the last king of the Fifth Dynasty, Unas, contains the first known example of the Pyramid Texts, which are hundreds of magic spells to help the dead king navigate the dangers of the underworld on his way to paradise.

During the Fifth Dynasty, power was somewhat decentralized and nomarchs and provincial nobles became increasingly wealthy and powerful. Many local posts became hereditary, with fathers passing power and tax-free estates to their sons. A feudal system developed, especially in Upper Egypt. Local rulers controlled mini-kingdoms and paid little attention to dictates from Memphis. As long as Egypt remained peaceful and taxes rolled in to the royal treasuries, the kings went along with this arrangement.

The Square Sail

Travel south to north in Egypt was always easy because that is the direction in which the Nile River flows. But north to south travel was slow and cumbersome until a clever boatman had a brainstorm around 3350 B.C.E. He attached a large square of fabric (probably linen) to a yard (a horizontal pole) that was attached to a mast near the front of his Nile boat. This sail caught the prevailing north-to-south winds and propelled his boat upriver.

Square sails are very inefficient if conditions require much steering and tacking (sailing on a zigzag into the wind). But since the Nile is relatively straight, calm, and easy to navigate, Egyptian sailors saw no need to improve much upon this invention. The little steering that was required needed only a steering pole or the use of slender steering oars. The square sail served them well for thousands of years.

When Egyptian sailors ventured into the Mediterranean Sea, or into the Red Sea down the coast of Africa to Punt (on the eastern coast of Africa, in the area of modern Somalia) even their seagoing ships were still fitted with simple square sails.

Later sailors, such as the Greeks and Phoenicians, faced with the more complex demands of sailing across the Mediterranean Sea, made numerous improvements to the square sail. They also developed more efficient sails in a variety of designs to more effectively catch the winds and propel large, heavy ships through deep water. But the basic shape of all square sails originally came from those ancient Nile reed boats.

Today, sailboats are still commonly used to carry goods and passengers along the Nile.

But there was rumbling on the borders. Soldiers often had to be sent to Nubia to protect trade routes and to recruit mercenaries (soldiers for hire) for the army and police forces. A major fort was established at Buhen, near the second cataract. Libyan raiders made repeated incursions from the western desert.

The Fifth Dynasty ended in confusion. The first king of the Sixth Dynasty, Teti, settled things down. But the power and influence of the king was severely declining. Local nobles no longer felt it necessary or even desirable to be buried near the king. They built tombs for themselves and their families in their own districts.

The last known king of the Old Kingdom, Pepy II, took the throne when he was a child. (Pepy II was, in fact, a Sixth Dynasty king, and the Old Kingdom ended in the Eighth Dynasty. However, not much is known about the kings of Dynasties 7 and 8, and Pepy II is the last king from this period to have had much influence over the course of events in the Old Kingdom.) His 94-year reign appears to have been marked by a steady decline in royal power. As the power of central government decreased, the power of local rulers increased. Instability and civil disorder followed Pepy's death.

A few hundred years of gloriously high culture had been followed by a severe backlash. Many scholars believe the artistic and architectural achievements of the Old Kingdom were never equaled. But the Great Pyramid and similar projects were enormous drains on Egypt's resources. The royal pretensions that led to such projects got out of hand. When powerful and all-too-independent nobles rebelled against the king's authority and a series of low Niles brought widespread crop failure and famine, pyramid-building was the last thing on the king's mind.

The First Intermediate Period

The god-king no longer enjoyed exalted status. Local rulers and nomarchs had grabbed much of his authority. When the collapse finally came, it was sudden and complete.

While general disorder and the independence of local rulers helped bring about the collapse of the Old Kingdom, many scholars believe that climate change in Africa and the Near East had at least as much to do with it. Changes in the patterns of monsoon rains over the Abyssinian highlands caused widespread drought and a series of low Niles. Food production abruptly declined. Hot winds blew from the south for weeks at a time, according to some ancient texts. Sandstorms and dust storms hid the sun for days. Already dry farms turned to dust. In some places, the Nile was so shallow that it could be crossed on foot. Drought and famine in the Near East drove bands of starving, desperate refugees to Egypt's borders, putting additional pressure on food and water supplies.

These disastrous events called into serious question the god-king's ability to control the river and to ensure agricultural success. The king quickly lost any reputation he still had for magical powers. Only local warlords had the power to repel invaders, control distribution of scarce food, and enforce water conservation. Egypt quickly splintered into numerous small feudal kingdoms ruled by powerful chieftains. Their only concerns were keeping their domains secure and keeping invaders out. Art, tomb building, and everything else had to wait.

This period spans from about 2130 B.C.E. to 1980 B.C.E., Dynasties 9 to 11 (early). But in fact, there is little information and much confusion about the length of this period (estimates range from 140 to 200 years) and the number of kings. A rapid succession of kings (sometimes more than one at a time) claimed the throne. None of these self-proclaimed rulers had much influence beyond Memphis. By 20 years after Pepy II's death, the Delta had been invaded by "Asiatics"—refugees and nomadic tribes from northeast of Egypt in the Near East, Palestine, and beyond, to the Tigris-Euphrates Valley. Egypt's government, such as it was, fled south.

One powerful faction ruled the Delta during the ninth and tenth dynasties, and parts of Middle Egypt from Herakleopolis. They brought a temporary end to warfare, expelled Asiatic invaders from the Delta, fortified the eastern borders, improved irrigation systems, and reestablished Memphis as a regional capital. Another powerful ruling family (the Eleventh Dynasty) ruled from Thebes. There were frequent border clashes between the Thebans and Herakleopolitans.

The Middle Kingdom

After years of fighting, the family in Thebes prevailed. They reunited Egypt under Mentuhotep II, leader of the last phase of the struggle against the Herakleopolitans. On becoming king, Mentuhotep took the kingly title "He who gives heart to the two lands." (This kingly title was called a Horus-name, after Horus, the falcon-headed god who was the traditional protector of Egyptian kings. The king is the physical embodiment of Horus-on-earth. To the ancient Egyptians, he *was* Horus.) In his 14th year of rule, he crushed a major rebellion in Abydos, securing his control of Upper Egypt. He changed his Horus-name to "Lord of the white crown."

Timekeeping and Shadow Clocks

The Egyptians were among the first people to subdivide the daylight and nighttime periods into smaller increments. They kept track of these with primitive but clever shadow clocks, precursors of sundials.

Many obelisks served as shadow clocks. The moving shadows cast by these tall, slender, tapering, four-sided monuments, which date from as early as 3500 B.C.E., enabled observers to divide the daylight hours into morning and afternoon. Marks on the ground nearby recorded the lengths of the shadows at various times of the year. On the longest day of the year, the shadow at noon was at its shortest length of the year. Other ground marks near the obelisk's base indicated smaller subdivisions of time.

The Egyptians may also have developed the world's first portable timepiece—ancestor of modern watches. A 14-inch-long bar with an elevated crosspiece, this device, dating from around 1500 B.C.E., divided a sunny day into 10 parts, plus two twilight hours—morning and evening. By facing east and orienting this timepiece east and west in the morning, the observer could read the time from the shadow cast by the crosspiece across five measured markings on the bar. After noon, he would face west and read the time from shadows cast in the opposite direction.

Timekeeping at night was a later innovation. Around 600 B.C.E., Egyptians developed a device called the *merkhet*, one of the world's oldest known astronomical tools. An observer aligned a pair of *merkhets* with the Pole Star to establish a meridian (a north-south line). By observing when other stars crossed this meridian, he could accurately track the hours of darkness.

It was not until his 39th year of rule that he reunited Upper and Lower Egypt. He changed his Horus-name to "Uniter of the two lands." So began the Middle Kingdom, which lasted 350 years and encompassed Dynasties 11 (late) to 14 (1980 B.C.E. to 1630 B.C.E.).

With strong central control, peace and prosperity returned. Mentuhotep II, ruling from Thebes, built a temple-tomb for himself at Deir el-Bahari, west of the city. He handed on to his son, Mentuhotep III, a stable, united Egypt.

Mentuhotep II and the kings who followed faced a new Egypt—one that had experienced chaos and misery. For the rest of the dynastic era, the suffering of the First Intermediate Period was remembered as a warning about what happens when order breaks down.

Faced with a growing population (perhaps 1.5 million people by 2000 B.C.E.), Middle Kingdom kings concentrated on expanding trade and agriculture, promoting the welfare of the country and keeping the peace. Unlike the all-powerful god-kings of the Old Kingdom, Middle Kingdom rulers could not harness the entire wealth of the nation to build lavish tombs. Pyramid building was revived during the Middle Kingdom, but they were not as large as the ones of the Old Kingdom. Instead of building lavish tombs, they devoted their attention and resources to repairs, land reclamation, irrigation, and harbors. They strengthened border defenses, dealing quickly and firmly with incursions by Libyans and Bedouins.

They renewed long-neglected diplomatic and trading relationships. Ambassadors and trade expeditions traveled to the ancient Phoenician city of Byblos, and other cities in the Near East, as well as Nubia and Punt. A new middle class of independent professionals, artisans, and tradesmen arose. Many farmers owned their own land, weakening the old system of feudal estates.

Secular (non-religious) literature—stories, poetry, songs, satires, proverbs, and wisdom literature (proverbs, collections of wise sayings, morality tales, fables, and advice to the young from their elders)—became popular. Stories called pessimistic literature reminded Egyptians about the misery of civil war, lest they forget.

With Thebes now the capital, the traditional Theban god Amun became prominent. He merged with Heliopolis's sun god Re, becoming Amun-Re. The Theban kings provided lavish support and rich gifts to Amun-Re's priesthood and temples.

Unlike the all-powerful god-kings of the Old Kingdom, Middle Kingdom rulers could not harness the entire wealth of the nation to build lavish tombs. Pyramid building was revived during the Middle Kingdom, but they wree not as large as the ones of the Old Kingdom.

The rapidly-growing cult of Osiris promised even poor peasants a pleasant afterlife. The Pyramid Texts were updated to apply to the wider range of spirits now eligible for eternal life. The revised spells, called the Coffin Texts, were painted or carved on wooden coffins. The new middle class of artisans started mass-producing grave goods: pottery, *ushabtis*, *serdab* statues (small statues of a dead person, sealed into a niche or chamber in the tomb), furniture, models, and more.

The Governor of the South and vizier of Mentuhotep IV overthrew his king to become Amenemhet I, founder of the Twelfth Dynasty. His 29-year reign gave Egypt its first extended period of stability and security in more than 200 years. His first move was to build and furnish a boat to cruise the Nile, putting nomarchs in their place and crushing troublesome Asiatics and Nubians.

To consolidate his power over Upper and Lower Egypt at a more strategic location, Amenemhet I established a new capital at Itj-tawy, about 20 miles south of Memphis. He introduced "co-regency" (a king sharing power with his heir) to strengthen royal succession and eliminate the instability that often followed a king's death. Co-regency made royal transitions much smoother, and was adopted by several later kings. Amenemhet shared the throne with his son, Senwosret, for 10 years. Senwosret handled the military and kept the frontiers secure. He established fortified towns and trading posts as far south as the third cataract.

When Senwosret I took the throne, he continued his military activities, securing Egypt's southern border at the second cataract with 13 forts. He sent mining expeditions to Nubia, Syria, and the western oases. He built a magnificent solar temple at Heliopolis.

The 34-year reign of his son, Amenemhet II, saw great achievements. The king widened and deepened the canal that fed the Faiyum from the Nile, expanding hunting, fishing, and agriculture. He sent trade expeditions to Punt, the Red Sea, Lebanon, and the Levant. He carried on a thriving trade with the Mediterranean island of Crete.

Senwosret II, son of Amenemhet II, presided over a peaceful, prosperous Egypt. He expanded cultivation in the Faiyum and established friendly (perhaps too friendly) relations with the nomarchs. His habit of giving them tax-free land grants and other rich gifts was one that had caused trouble before. His son, Senwosret III, decided to nip that problem in the bud once and for all. He created a new government structure that greatly minimized the power of the nomarchs. He closed their courts and revoked their rights and privileges. The new government had three major departments: North, South, and Elephatine/Nubia. Each was overseen by a council of senior officials reporting to a department vizier, who reported directly to the king.

During his 18-year reign, Senwosret III showed remarkable skill in managing economic affairs and foreign policy. He led a series of military campaigns to secure Nubian trade routes, protect the southern borders, secure access to the gold mines, and suppress troublesome Nubians. He cut a bypass canal around the first cataract, improving on a primitive Old Kingdom canal. This allowed speedier, safer trade, and rapid movement of soldiers to trouble spots. Senwosret also built many forts along the southern frontier.

Senwosret's relations with Asia were mostly peaceful trading partnerships, though he did do some plundering. Much of the plunder and trade wealth that flowed in went to support the temples of Amun-Re at Thebes.

The next king, Amenemhet III, enjoyed 46 years of peace, prosperity, economic growth, and high artistic achievement. He sent almost continual expeditions to the turquoise mines of the Sinai to satisfy Egypt's endless desire for this prized gemstone.

Amenemhet III built two pyramids for himself. One he abandoned. The other, where he was buried, is famous for the large number of features designed to keep tomb robbers out. There were trap doors, false passages and dead ends. His sarcophagus was carved from a single, massive block of quartzite. After his burial, it was topped with a 45-ton stone slab, and all passages and corridors were filled with rock and rubble. His tomb was looted anyway.

Little is known about the last two Middle Kingdom rulers who are named and known, Amenemhet IV and Queen Sobeknefru. Climate change was causing instability in the inundation—the river was always either too high or too low. The resulting disruption led to Egypt's second extended period of disorder, the Second Intermediate Period. Egypt was about to experience her worst nightmare: rule by foreigners.

Egypt entered a period of internal instability, though not as long or severe as the First Intermediate Period. The Thirteenth Dynasty, ruling from Itj-tawy, included many kings with brief reigns. They maintained some control over both Upper and Lower Egypt, but left few monuments or records. A competing faction (the Fourteenth Dynasty) ruled from a power base in the western Delta. It included an unknown number of obscure kings who came and went quickly. Egyptian control of Nubia collapsed, but many Egyptians stayed to work for local Nubian rulers.

As the 13th and 14th dynasties struggled with one another, a group of foreigners of Semitic origin claimed dominion over Egypt from their eastern Delta power base, Avaris. The Hyksos soon controlled the eastern Delta and the eastern deserts.

The Hyksos had been clever. They did not invade with fanfare and drawn swords. Instead, they immigrated into the eastern Delta and settled in, waiting for the right moment to make their move. Their political influence was largely confined to the Delta. The five (or six) Hyksos kings adopted Egyptian titles, dress, and traditions. They worshiped traditional Egyptian gods and goddesses (they preferred Seth over Osiris), while introducing several of their own to the religious mix. They built many temples and sponsored developments in Egyptian arts, crafts, and literature. They sacked Memphis, but did not cause the widespread terror and destruction claimed by later writers.

The Second Intermediate Period

The horror of having their throne seized by foreigners caused the Egyptians to see the Hyksos in the worst possible light. But in many ways, Hyksos rule was the best thing that could have happened to Egypt. It rescued Egypt from political turmoil and cultural decline. The Hyksos brought fresh ideas and new technologies to a land that had become fixed in its outlook.

They introduced Egypt to superior bronze-age technology, already in wide use elsewhere. They introduced new military strategies, tactics, and equipment: the chariot and horse, the composite bow, scale armor (armor with solid, overlapping tabs of metal, rather like metal fish scales), and improved daggers and swords. Without these innovations, it is doubtful Egypt could have become an imperial superpower.

The Hyksos also introduced fresh ideas to the arts and everyday life. The vertical weaving loom, stringed musical instruments (lute and lyre), the oboe, the tambourine, the olive and pomegranate trees—all came to Egypt with the Hyksos. This 107-year period (1630 to 1539 B.C.E.) spans Dynasties 15 to 17.

Egypt had always been strongly inward-looking. Egyptians had not seen the outside world as threatening, or even as very interesting or important. It was a handy shopping mall where they could get things they

Models and Magic

The tomb of Meketre, chancellor to Eleventh Dynasty king Mentuhotep II, held a secret missed by the looters who otherwise stripped it. In a sealed chamber, Meketre had placed 25 exquisitely detailed models of daily life and activities that his spirit could magically activate to brew his afterlife beer, catch fish for him, clean his house, serve his meals, bake his bread, haul water, care for his animals, fight off invaders, weave linen, build him a Nile yacht—any task that would need doing in the afterlife.

A model of the cattle census is complete with animals, herdsmen, village officials, and royal tax collectors. There are models of granaries (buildings for storing grain), boats of different sizes, and Meketre's house and garden.

There are miniature workshops for bakers, butchers, brewers, weavers, and woodworkers Meketre added model serving girls to carry water, and battalions of tiny archers and soldiers, ready to fight if the need arose. Some of the models from Meketre's tomb can be seen at the Metropolitan Museum of Art in New York City (the rest are in the Cairo Museum).

The tradition of placing such models, and other servant figures, such as *ushabtis* ("answerers"), in tombs was a typical Egyptian response to a practical problem. With fewer resources available to build and stock huge, lavish tombs, even the king relied on magical servant figures, and paintings, figurines, and menus that could be magically activated as needed.

wanted. Seeing their kingship seized by foreigners finally opened their eyes. The Hyksos takeover profoundly changed the Egyptians' view of the world. They realized they needed to do more than just go shopping in the world's mines and bazaars. They needed a strong, even aggressive, foreign policy to prevent the many up-and-coming nations around the Mediterranean from coming in and taking whatever they wanted—including the throne. For the first time, Egypt established a standing army and a professional military. Because of the Hyksos, Egypt was no longer isolated from the world.

As the Hyksos consolidated control over the Delta, a family of Theban princes formed a ruling faction (the Seventeenth Dynasty) at Thebes. They preserved Middle Kingdom culture, and controlled Upper Egypt from Elephantine to Abydos, north of Thebes. The Hyksos and the Nubians, who had formed an alliance, hemmed in the Thebans for almost 100 years. Finally, simmering tensions exploded into open conflict.

The Thebans were determined to drive the hated foreigners off the throne and out of Egypt. King Seqenenre Tao and his son Kamose mounted fierce campaigns against the Hyksos. Seqenenre Tao was soon killed. His mummy shows terrible wounds, probably inflicted in battle. Kamose resumed the fight, retaking the Nubian border forts and leading a raid to the outskirts of Avaris. But he reigned only three years.

His son, Ahmose was also determined to drive the invaders out, but waited for the right moment. About halfway through his 26-year reign, he led attacks against the Hyksos at their strongholds in Avaris and Memphis. After a hard-fought campaign, Ahmose prevailed. Not content with driving the Hyksos out of Egypt, he chased them all the way back to Palestine and laid siege to their home city, which was in northern Palestine (what the Bible describes as Caanan).

The Theban ruling family became the Eighteenth Dynasty, and Ahmose I the first king of the New Kingdom. Egypt's glorious imperial age was about to begin.

CHAPTER 2

Imperial Egypt

THE 350 YEARS OF DYNASTIES 18 AND 19 WERE THE WORLD'S first great empire. A series of brilliant military pharaohs extended Egypt's domain from the fourth cataract deep in Nubia in the south, to the Euphrates River in the Near East. Egypt's empire was much smaller than the later Persian and Roman empires, was built up gradually, and took shape not entirely by design. Egypt's greatest general-kings appeared when much of the rest of the Mediterranean world was unstable and weak. Still, Egypt was the world's first superpower.

The imperial age brought vast wealth and a new, cosmopolitan outlook to Egypt. Previously isolated in their narrow valley, Egyptians now subdued a multitude of nations, adopted their gods and goddesses, and imported their fashions and technologies.

Sons of the leaders of conquered territories in Nubia and Asia were compelled to live in Egypt, study in temple schools, and learn Egyptian ways. Foreign princesses joined the royal harem—the king's group of wives. Harems could be quite large, with hundreds of wives. Although these foreigners lived in luxury, their marriages were strictly diplomatic—their presence kept the tribute and gifts flowing, and discouraged revolt.

Trade, always important, became more varied and extensive. Finely made products—weapons, furniture, faience (glazed earthenware), linen, jewelry—from the workshops of Egypt's skilled artisans were in demand everywhere. Goods and materials Egyptians had always craved poured in from abroad.

From Nubia and further south came gold, ebony, ivory, amethysts, carnelian, jasper, diorite (a hard, grayish-green stone used for statues), leopard skins and other exotic animal pelts, incense, oils, ostrich eggs

OPPOSITE
Sun Worshipers
The royal family of Akhenaten offers a sacrifice to Aten, the sun god, on this 1350 B.C.E. relief from Amarna. During Akhenaten's brief reign, Egypt had the first recorded monotheistic (belief in one god) religion.

and feathers, and monkeys. From the mountainous deserts to the east came carnelian, garnets, jasper, rock crystal, obsidian, green and multi-hued feldspar, alabaster, copper, and rare emeralds. The copper and turquoise mines of Sinai were in constant production. Silver and lapis lazuli came from the far reaches of the Near East.

With Ahmose's triumph over the Hyksos (see page 35), the Thebans reigned supreme. In a series of military campaigns, Ahmose secured Egypt's borders. To build support for his central government, he gave the nomarchs and provincial nobles a great deal of authority and responsibility—backed up with land grants and rich gifts. He also started major temple-building projects all over the country. His son, Amenhotep I, ruled for 21 years, continuing his father's military campaigns in Nubia and Syria, and founding the great temple of Karnak, near Thebes.

The next king, Thutmose I, was a non-royal general who gained the throne by marrying a princess. During his 11-year reign, the priests of Amun-Re at Thebes became fabulously wealthy and powerful.

Thutmose II was the son of a royal harem woman. He found it prudent to strengthen his claim to the throne by marrying his half-sister. Like Thutmose I, he conducted successful military campaigns in Nubia and Syria.

Thutmose III was also the son of a minor harem wife. He became king as a small child. His aunt Hatshepsut, ruling as his regent, seized the throne within two years. A talented and ambitious woman, Hatshepsut became one of Egypt's most powerful female pharaohs. She built and restored many temples, and built a splendid mortuary temple of unique design for herself at Deir el-Bahari near Thebes. With her lavish royal support, the Amun-Re priesthood became even richer.

Hatshepsut was not much concerned with military matters, but she was very interested in trade. She sent almost continuous expeditions to the turquoise mines of Sinai, and to Punt, down the African coast. Meanwhile, Thutmose III was in the army, studying military strategy and planning his comeback.

There is much historical evidence that Thutmose III disliked his aunt Hatshepsut. As soon as she died (some scholars speculate that Thutmose actually had a hand in her death), he destroyed many of her monuments and those of her supporters. He scratched her name off inscriptions and made sure she was left off the official king lists. His revenge complete, he proceeded to earn his modern title, "The Napoleon of Egypt."

THE PHARAOHS

The word *pharaoh* comes from the word *per-aa*, which is the Egyptian word for "great house" or "palace." Over time, the phrase "the Great House says . . ." came to mean "the king says . . ." just as "the White House says . . ." really means "the president says . . ." By the Eighteenth Dynasty, Great House, or Pharaoh, was one of the king's titles.

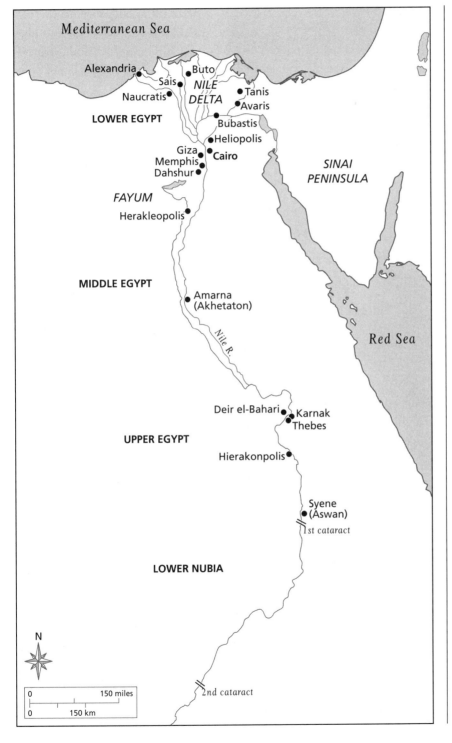

Egypt Is the Nile
The grandest and most important cities in imperial Egypt were clustered around the Nile River. In this mainly desert region of North Africa, the Nile meant life.

A Rare Likeness

Hatshepsut, the aunt of Thutmose II, became one of Egypt's most powerful female pharaohs. But after her death, her nephew had most evidence of her reign erased.

Building a Superpower

The first king to use ships for major troop movements, Thutmose III launched campaigns against Syria each summer for 18 years. In his most brilliant victory, he marched to Gaza in 10 days and took the city. He proceeded to Meggido and drove off the enemy after a daringly clever surprise attack.

Unfortunately, his soldiers could not resist the temptation to do some looting. This gave the enemy time to build up their defenses in Meggido. (A seven-month siege finally dislodged them.) Thutmose III conquered more than 350 cities in the Near East, from the northeast border of Egypt to the Euphrates River. The temples of Amun-Re got most of the spoils, as well as large shares of the tribute that flowed in from conquered provinces.

Thutmose I had already pretty much conquered Nubia, enabling Thutmose III to concentrate on Asia. His primary opponent was the Mittani Empire in northern Syria, which eventually fell to Egypt.

The court of Thutmose III was luxurious beyond anything we can imagine today. During his 54-year reign, nothing was too good for his hundreds of wives (including many foreign princesses) and military generals. Tombs and grave goods from his era are remarkable for their high quality and abundance.

Perfume and Cosmetics

A wealthy woman during Egypt's imperial age, dressed for a party or festival, might have stepped from the pages of a modern fashion magazine (except for that odd white cone atop her head). Her pleated, embroidered linen gown, fringed wool shawl, elaborate wig, and flashy jewelry would be the pride of a Paris designer.

Modern beauties would recognize her routine. She took a leisurely bath, washing with a refreshing solution of natron (a drying mineral) and fragrant oil. A cleansing cream made of oil mixed with lime (a mineral power) toned and softened her skin. She applied a wrinkle-fighting potion, custom-made from a secret recipe from the king's personal physician.

She rubbed a deodorant made of ground carob (crushed pods from the carob tree, with a chocolate fragrance) onto her body. An edible perfume of natron, cinnamon oils, and a "secret ingredient" from Punt sweetened her breath.

She opened her make-up kit, surveying tiny jars of gold, translucent stone, ivory, and glass in the shapes of animals and birds, filled with powders, oils, unguents, and perfumes. (Unlike modern alcohol-based perfumes, hers were oil-based, scented with exotic ingredients such as cinnamon, myrrh, frankincense, cardamom, wine, and honey.) She selected a miniature gold spoon for mixing oils, her carved black kohl stick, several make-up palettes, and a pol-ished copper hand mirror carved in the form of Hathor, the goddess of beauty.

Using her kohl stick, she applied thick black lines around her eyes. A touch more defined and lengthened her brows. She patted her cheeks with a dusting of powdered red ochre, then mixed a bit of it with oil to make colored lip gloss. She applied henna (a reddish dye extracted from the rose-scented loosetrife plant) to parts of her wig, her feet, the palms of her hands, and her fingernails.

Her servants helped her wiggle into a tight-fitting, pleated linen sheath, topped with an embroidered wool shawl. She donned her fashionably long, braided wig, adding a circlet (crown-shaped hair ornament) of gold with tiny gemstone flowers. From her over-flowing jewelry case, she selected heavy gold earrings with dangling beads, several rings (one shaped like the ankh, symbol for life), and a three-row beaded collar of gold, turquoise, lapis lazuli, and amethyst. Finally, she donned five gold bracelets—one on each upper arm and three for her dainty wrists.

At the door, she slipped into delicate leather sandals decorated with fresh flowers. She added a few fresh flowers to her wig. Just before leaving, she placed a cone of scented fat atop her wig. Over the evening, the heat would gradually melt the fat, releasing its scent and running a cooling stream of perfume down her wig, face, and neck.

The Amarna Period

In his third year of rule, Amenhotep IV held a *heb-sed*, a traditional festival that re-affirmed his fitness to rule. Oddly, no gods except his favorite, the Aten, were included. The Aten, a winged sun disk, was an obscure god in whom Amenhotep's parents had taken an interest, but only as one god among many. The *heb-sed* shrines featured only Amenhotep IV beneath the Aten disk. Even Amun-Re was excluded.

By his fifth year as ruler, Amenhotep had promoted the Aten to official state god. Support that used to flow to Amun-Re temples and priests went to the Aten cult, which quickly grew rich. Temples of Amun-Re closed for lack of funds. The king declared that the Aten was the one true god, and banned all others—a staggering change in a land where 2,000 gods were worshiped.

Amenhotep changed his name to Akhenaten ("Living Spirit of the Aten") and moved his capital to a new city, Akhetaten ("Horizon of the Aten") on the east bank of the Nile, halfway between Thebes and Memphis—modern Tell el-Amarna. The brief era of Akhenaten's radical religious upheaval is called the Amarna Period.

Within four years, Akhetaten, the city, was fully functional. It became both the religious and political capital of Egypt. Buildings were decorated with art in the new Amarna style, with charming scenes of Akhenaten, the king, his wife Nefertiti (which means "a beautiful woman has come"), and their six daughters.

The elite found it wise to swiftly convert. But almost everyone else continued to quietly worship their traditional gods and goddesses. The Aten religion, actually a cult formed around the personality of the king, never caught on outside the king's closed circle.

In the 12th year of Akhenaten's reign, several members of his family died suddenly, possibly of plague. Nefertiti vanished. She may have died, or she may have been "retired" because she produced no sons. Akhenaten married at least one of his surviving daughters—but still got no sons. He became increasingly intolerant of the persistent interest in the old gods, traditional religion, and anybody who disagreed with his radical religious notions. After ruling for 17 years, he died.

Massive confusion followed. The identity of his immediate successor is a hot topic of scholarly controversy. Tutankhaten, the king who followed the mystery successor, changed his name to Tutankhamun and moved the capital back to Thebes. He demolished the Aten's temples, and erased the names of Akhenaten and Nefertiti from monuments. Amun-Re ruled once more.

Akhetaten was abandoned. With its residents gone and valuables removed, it sank back into the desert sands, until it was rediscovered by archaeologists in the early 1800s.

The kings who followed Akhenaten tried to erase the heretic king, his wife, and the entire embarrassing episode from history. In spite of their efforts, Akhenaten and Nefertiti are among the best-known icons of ancient Egypt—and the Amarna Period is one of the most intensively studied and fascinating eras of Egyptian history.

The death of Thutmose III provoked widespread revolts around his empire. Because Egypt had never been known for military or imperial ambitions, the conquered peoples could be forgiven for hoping that when Thutmose III died, they would be able to regain their independence. But his son, Amenhotep II, quickly set them straight. A vigorous man, famous as a sportsman and athlete, the new king subdued every revolt. He moved swiftly into Nubia, killing seven captive Nubian princes. He hung one from the walls of the Nubian capital, as a warning. A decisive campaign in Palestine confirmed that Amenhotep meant to hold on to his empire.

For the rest of his 26-year reign, peace ruled the empire. Tribute flowed into Egypt as reliably as the Nile floods. The next king, Thutmose IV, also enjoyed a peaceful, prosperous reign. Thutmose IV and the powerful Mittani kingdom of the Near East reached a peace accord, and Thutmose married at least one Mittani princess. From then on, all that was required to keep the empire in line were a few "police actions" in Nubia and Syria.

The next king, Amenhotep III presided over a prosperous, stable empire. There was little need for military action during his 37-year reign, because the empire was secure. Egypt was the world's undisputed superpower. The king built grand temples, enhanced his reputation as a sportsman, and enjoyed luxury and high living at his fabulous court, along with more than 1,000 wives. His era is known for magnificent artwork and statuary.

Egypt's wealth during this prosperous era did not come from war booty, but from vast international trade and tribute from conquered provinces. Gold poured in from the empire's mines. The king built a spectacular mortuary temple at Thebes that included two 60-foot-tall statues of himself, known as the colossi of Memnon.

It was lucky for Egypt that the next king reigned only 17 years. Focused on promoting his new religion, Amenhotep IV badly neglected the empire. Only quick, decisive work by the kings who followed him kept Egypt's empire together.

Tutankhamun was a young boy, and his power was controlled and manipulated by older, experienced officials. During his 10-year reign, extensive building was carried out at the temples of Karnak and Luxor. There were military campaigns in Nubia and Syria, although Tutankhamun probably did not personally participate. He left no heir. He may have been murdered, but this idea is very controversial.

Government Documents Never Change

To archaeologists' dismay, centuries of *sebakh* gatherers have destroyed all traces of many ancient settlements. On the plus side, it was a sebakh gatherer who found the Amarna Letters. This collection of documents, written in the cuneiform script of Mesopotamia, was discovered in 1887 at Tell el-Amarna. The discoverer tried to sell them, only to be told they were fakes. They are not.

The Amarna Letters are some of the most valuable documents ever found in ancient Egypt. They are personal and diplomatic correspondence between the court of Eighteenth Dynasty king Akhenaten and foreign kings and officials.

A modern diplomat would instantly recognize the subjects and tone of the letters: complaints about Egypt's foreign policy, demands for gifts or tribute, requests for special treatment, pleas for more foreign aid, insincere apologies for border raids, attempts to gain favor with flattery and praise, boring details of trade agreements. He would also recognize the muddled, rambling jargon typical of government documents—then and now.

Akhenaten's reign had destabilized the empire at a time when the neighboring Hittites were becoming a major force. Renewed military efforts would have been needed, but Tutankhamun had been too young and inexperienced to lead effective military campaigns. After Tutankhamun's premature death, his young wife, Ankhesenamun, wrote to the Hittite king and asked him to send one of his sons. She would marry the son, she said, and he would become king of Egypt.

This sounded too good to be true. The Hittite king suspected a trap, and sent a team of diplomats to investigate. Assured that Ankhesenamun's story was true and her offer sincere, the Hittite sent his son—who was ambushed at the border and murdered. The next three generations saw sporadic war between Egypt and the Hittites.

Tutankhamun's successor, Ay, was an elderly official who had served under several kings. Ay ruled only four years. He was followed by

Horemheb, an experienced, war-hardened general whom scholars consider the chief suspect in the murder of the unfortunate Hittite prince. Horemheb was a career officer who had served ably under three kings. Supremely ambitious, he seized the throne upon Ay's death, and married a sister of Nefertiti to establish a link to the royal family.

There is little evidence that Horemheb undertook any major military campaigns. His 27-year reign was focused on restoration, consolidation, internal reforms, and rewriting history. He immediately repaired and reopened temples closed by Akhenaten. He restored the wealth and prestige of the Amun-Re temples with lavish royal support—but took the precaution of appointing army officers loyal to him as chief priests. He did everything possible to erase all records of the kings between Amenhotep III and himself.

After Horemheb's death, his vizier became king. Ramesses I, first king of the Nineteenth Dynasty, was a career military officer who reigned only two years. His son, Sety I, presided over a rebirth of art and culture. A major builder and patron of Amun-Re, Sety I started the splendid Great Hypostyle Hall at the temple of Karnak, and built many other temples. He also resumed military campaigns to Nubia and Syria. His tomb is the largest and finest in the Valley of the Kings. But his greatest achievement might have been fathering Ramesses II—Ramesses the Great.

Ramesses II did everything on the grandest possible scale. No other pharaoh built so many temples, fathered so many children (more than 100 sons, daughters not counted), or erected so many colossal statues and obelisks. He presided over the peak of Egypt's imperial age.

As a young prince, Ramesses II participated in many military campaigns against the Hittites. Soon after taking the throne, he led 20,000 soldiers against the Hittites in a great battle at Kadesh in Syria. The battle ended in a stalemate, but Ramesses II returned home and proclaimed victory. Further campaigns had similar outcomes. This started getting expensive, and embarrassing, for both sides. According to Egyptian records, it was the Hittite king who proposed a peace treaty. Hittite records say it was Ramesses. In any case, flowery diplomatic letters, rich royal gifts, and Ramesses's marriage to a Hittite princess sealed the peace pact.

Ramesses II was one of Egypt's biggest builders. He completed Sety's mortuary temple at Thebes, another for himself at Abydos, and the huge mortuary temple called the Ramesseum. He added to the temple complexes Karnak and Luxor, and built major temples all over Egypt. His Great Temple at Abu Simbel, cut into the rocky cliffs near Elephantine, was dedicated to the gods Re-Herakhte, Ptah, and Amon-Re—but with its four 60-foot-tall statues of himself, it was clearly meant to proclaim his own magnificence. Nearby, he built a smaller temple to honor his favorite wife, Nefertari, and the goddess Hathor. He built a new city, Piramesse ("Domain of Ramesses") in the Delta.

A total of 14 jubilee festivals were held in ancient Egypt by various kings. Also called *heb-sed* festivals, these weeks-long national parties were held to reaffirm the king's vigor and fitness to rule. The *heb-sed* included many religious ceremonies and a ritual "marathon run" in which the king ran a course around the temple precincts to show that he was in excellent shape. Kings held *heb-seds* at different intervals, and some held many more than others. They were generally 10 to 15 years apart during the 64-year reign of Ramesses II. The king was more than 90 years old when he died.

Ramesses II is believed by many scholars to be "Pharaoh" mentioned in the Bible in the book of Exodus, which describes how Moses freed the Israelite people from Egyptian slavery. However, there are no surviving records in Egypt of this event during the reign of any pharaoh.

The Beginning of the End

When Merneptah, 13th son of Ramesses II, took the throne, revolt was in the air. Merneptah repelled waves of Libyan invaders, subdued rebellion in Nubia, and turned back hordes of refugees from Mesopotamia, who were suffering from extreme droughts. (He did send grain to the famine-stricken Hittites.) Times were equally difficult for the rulers who followed him through the end of the Nineteenth Dynasty, including Twosret, Egypt's fourth reigning queen. Within 25 years of the death of Ramesses the Great, Egypt was beset by invaders, and disorder mounted. The Nineteenth Dynasty ended in confusion.

The Twentieth Dynasty saw the beginning of the end of Egypt's empire. Ramesses III was the last great imperial pharaoh. When he took the throne in 1279 B.C.E., the world was in turmoil. The Trojan War and the fall of Mycenae in what is today Greece, and several years of drought, poor harvests, and famine in lands around the Mediterranean sent hordes of refugees on the move.

A confederation of refugees—collectively called the Sea Peoples—tried again to invade Egypt. They had first appeared during the reign of Merneptah, but had been turned back. This was not an army. These were entire nations—men, women, children, animals, household goods—on the

CONNECTIONS >>>>>>>>>>>>>>>>>>>>>>>>>>>>>>>>>>>

Holding up the Sky

Even before the dawn of the Old Kingdom, Egyptian architects were using columns to span large spaces and hold up roofs. They were the first builders to do so. The earliest columns were faithful copies of the palm tree trunks and bound bundles of branches and logs that Egyptians had long used to support the reed and rush roofs of their dwellings. The earliest columns in stone or brick were carefully constructed and carved to closely mimic the sizes, shapes and textures of their organic models.

The earliest builders may have believed that trees held up roofs by some kind of magic, and so thought it wise to imitate their forms as closely as possible when using other materials. Conservative in architecture as in everything else, Egyptians were not comfortable straying too far from the way things had always been done. Because they knew trees and bound bundles of plant materials would hold up roofs, it made sense to model all roof support structures after these proven forms.

By the Fifth Dynasty, Egyptians were building graceful, elaborate, granite and limestone columns modeled after palm trees, complete with crowns of palm foliage. Other columns resembled bound bundles of papyrus stalks, crowned with clusters of buds. Later columns recalled the lotus flower, either fully opened with outstretched petals or in bud.

Greek travelers to Egypt were awestruck by the magnificent colonnades (rows and groups of columns) in Egyptian temples. Inscribed, decorated, colorfully painted, and topped with stone flowers and foliage, these Egyptian columns found their way, somewhat transformed, into Greek architecture. Whenever you see a modern bank, government building, or stately mansion fronted by a row of graceful columns, thank an ancient Egyptian architect.

move, desperate for a place to live. They had their eyes on the fertile Nile River Delta.

Their attempts to invade overland were met with fierce resistance, resulting in heavy loss of life. When their ships approached close to Egypt's northern shore, ranks of archers drove them off with wave after wave of deadly arrows. The remnants of the Sea Peoples were finally chased back to the Near East.

This gave Egypt only a short break from trouble. Invasions of the Delta and several waves of Libyan invaders required the king's attention. Ramesses III crushed them all. His reign was prosperous, but troubled. He was even beset by problems in his own palace. A "harem conspiracy," led by a minor queen who wanted to promote her son's fortunes (and her

Elegant Support

The earliest columns in Egyptian buildings were copies of palm tree trunks. Later columns were even more elaborate, using stylized renderings of papyrus and lotus plants.

own) plotted to kill the king. The plot was discovered just in time. Most of the conspirators were allowed to commit suicide (considered a great boon) in lieu of execution. A few other chose to kill themselves rather than face lesser punishments, such as having their ears and noses chopped off.

Ramesses III was followed by a long series of kings, also named Ramesses (IV through XI). They are called the Ramessides. The kings from Ramesses IV onward had no family connection with Ramesses the Great. And borrowing his name did them little good. Little is known about these kings. During the 81 years of their reigns, internal instability increased. Trade dropped sharply. Egypt was plagued by civil wars, strikes, widespread lawlessness, and huge price increases. The empire was swiftly receding, which meant less tribute and gifts coming in (the Egyptian economy and the lifestyles of the rich and royal had become quite dependent upon all this tribute, which they did not have to work to earn). Troubles around the Mediterranean curtailed trade, meaning even less income. The pie was shrinking and the elites were elbowing one another to get their share before it all disappeared. The growing prevalence of in-fighting was not good for social stability. Nubia, and its important gold re-sources, was finally lost. Under Ramesses VI, the eastern frontier was pulled back to the eastern Delta. The turquoise mines in the Sinai were abandoned. Some building still went on in Egypt, but as less tribute flowed in from the weakening empire, funds dried up.

The powerful priests of Amun-Re at Thebes rebelled openly against the throne. Civil war raged in Thebes. Finally, Herihor, a high priest of Amun-Re who had risen through the military ranks and had been south-ern vizier and viceroy of Nubia, declared himself king. His reign over-lapped the last six years of the reign of Ramesses XI, who continued to rule from Piramesse in the Delta. The two kings acknowledged each others' sep-arate spheres of influence. There was not much Ramesses XI could do about it.

CHAPTER 3

Egypt's Long Decline

THE FLOWERING OF EGYPTIAN CULTURE WAS COMING TO AN end. When Ramesses XI died, Smendes, a relative of the Theban priests, became king in the north and founded the Twenty-first Dynasty.

The Third Intermediate Period

This period covers Dynasties 21 through 25, spanning 419 years from 1075 B.C.E. to 664 B.C.E.. Smendes moved his capital from Piramesse to Tanis, in the eastern Delta. The Tanite kings (who ruled only the Delta) and the Theban kings recognized each other's separate rights of succession, respected one another's power, and cemented ties between their families with royal marriages. Both ruling families had strong Libyan roots, and both kings were considered legitimate. But Egypt, with a population approaching 3 million, suffered from the lack of strong central government.

For most of the Twenty-first Dynasty, the Tanite kings in the Delta and the Theban soldier-priest-kings in the rest of Egypt were closely related. Sometimes they were brothers. The Theban king Pinedjem married one of the daughters of Ramesses XI. One of Pinedjem's sons, Psusennes I, became the third king of the Tanis Dynasty. Two other sons became priest-kings, ruling from Thebes. The daughter of Psusennes I married the high priest of Amun-Re, further linking the ruling families. A great temple at Tanis was dedicated to the Theban gods Amun-Re, Mut, and Khonsu.

During his 25-year reign at Tanis (coinciding with the Biblical era of David and Goliath), King Siamun built extensively at both Tanis and Piramesse. Also during that time, Egyptian princesses started marrying foreign princes and kings, reversing a long-held pattern.

OPPOSITE
Classic Beauty
This Egyptian beauty is Cleopatra VII (69–30 B.C.E.). She became queen at the age of 17, and was the last ruler of an independent Egypt until the 20th century.

The Theban priest-kings, well aware of tomb robberies in the Valley of the Kings, worried that the great pharaohs buried there were losing out on eternal life. They removed many royal mummies from their original tombs (many had already been looted) and stashed them in large groups in well-hidden, better-secured tombs. They also removed just about all the gold, valuables, and grave goods they found, "recycling" the loot into their temple treasuries, or saving it for their own tombs.

Two of these caches of royal mummies were discovered in the late 1800s by European explorers. One cache was discovered in 1881 in a tomb at Deir el-Bahari near Thebes, another in 1898 in the tomb of Amenhotep II in the Valley of the Kings. Dozens of royal mummies—including most of Egypt's great imperial pharaohs—had been packed into small chambers, side by side, with only the linen on their backs.

Some of their recycled funeral goods showed up in the tomb of Psusennes I—the only completely intact royal tomb ever found in Egypt. Psusennes had a solid silver coffin trimmed with gold, and a solid gold face mask. His sarcophagus, coffins, and other burial equipment had clearly belonged to other kings. The borrowed finery did his mummy little good; poor conditions in his tomb destroyed it.

Little is known about Psusennes II, last king of the Twenty-first Dynasty. His son, Shoshenq I, founded the Twenty-second Dynasty, also known as the Libyan or Bubastite Dynasty because the kings of the Twenty-second Dynasty were descended from Libyan raiders who had invaded Egypt during the reigns of Meneptah and Ramesses III and settled in the eastern Delta at Bubastis. They ruled Egypt for 233 years.

Shoshenq I took the title great chief of the Meshwesh Libyans. He led a campaign against Palestine (he is the ruler Shishak mentioned in the Bible), plundering Solomon's temple and looting everything but the Ark of the Covenant. This bold raid restored some of Egypt's old prestige. A strong leader, Shoshenq I reunited Upper and Lower Egypt, and kept them together for nearly 100 years.

Despite this, there was plenty of internal conflict. The power of the Tanis faction weakened, and the north splintered in many hereditary fiefdoms that paid little attention to the king. In the south, a patchwork of small kingdoms arose. By the time Shoshenq III took the throne, Egypt had entered the most confusing period in her long history.

During the Twenty-third Dynasty, Upper and Lower Egypt split apart. Factions fought over control of the Delta. During this so-called "Libyan anarchy," nine major kingdoms (collectively called the Twenty-third Dynasty) coexisted. This fragmentation seriously weakened Egypt, leaving it unable to defend itself from the Nubians, who swept north. By the end of the dynasty, at least three or four rulers claimed to be king of Egypt. Too late, they saw the threat from Nubia.

One self-proclaimed king, Tefnakhte, ruling from Sais in the Delta (the Twenty-fourth Dynasty), tried to organize a coalition of Upper and Lower Egyptian rulers to fight the Nubian invasion. The forces of the north met the Nubian forces at Herakleopolis. The northerners were forced to surrender, but Nubian king Piankhy allowed them to remain as governors of their cities. A second Sais king, Bakenrenef (Bocchoris) rebelled. The Nubians killed him.

The Twenty-fifth Dynasty was the Nubian Dynasty. Nubia was a stable, prosperous, completely Egyptianized state. Long a colony of Egypt, the Nubians treasured ancient Egyptian culture. Believing that Egypt had lost her way, they did not see themselves as invaders, but as restorers of the old order. They took the titles of great New Kingdom pharaohs, and maintained traditional Egyptian religion and culture. For 104 years, they ruled Egypt from Memphis and Thebes. They worshiped Amun-Re, rebuilt and refurbished neglected temples and monuments, and built many new temples. Imitating the ancient pharaohs, the Nubian kings built pyramid tombs

Nubian Renaissance

Nubia has long been closely linked with Egypt. Ancient Egypt subdued Nubia, sometimes cruelly, in order to keep gold mines and southern trade routes open. Nubians and others (sometimes convicted criminals) worked the mines under horrendous, near-slavery conditions. Over long years as a colony of Egypt, though, the Nubians came to admire and imitate Egyptian culture. For about 100 years, during the Twenty-fifth Dynasty, Nubian kings ruled Egypt.

Nubia also maintained strong cultural ties with Sub-Saharan Africa. After the Aswan High Dam was built in 1965, the Nile's annual flood built up behind the dam. By 1971, much of ancient Nubia was flooded, drowned forever beneath Lake Nasser. Anthropologists sadly proclaimed the end of Nubian culture.

However, instead of fading into history, the Nubians migrated into Cairo, bringing their culture, language, dress, and music with them. Nubian music, modernized with electric instruments added to traditional ones, has taken Egyptian pop music culture by storm. Anthropologists learned that it is a mistake to count out people who once transformed themselves from mine slaves into pharaohs.

Animal Cults

Animal cults were always important in Egyptian religion. This fascinated some observers, such as Herodotus, but horrified others. "Who does not know what monsters are adored by demented Egypt?" wrote Roman poet and satirist Juvenal in 127 C.E. in his *Fifteenth Satire* (as quoted in John Manchip White's *Ancient Egypt: Its Culture and History*).

The Egyptians did not actually worship animals. They worshiped the god or goddess who resided in the animal's form. Many of these deities were depicted with the animal's head on a human body.

One animal cult that was widely popular among all classes of people centered on the bull. In different parts of Egypt, the sacred bull was known by different names, and even represented different gods. The Apis bull was the god Ptah at Memphis; the Mnevis bull was the god Re at Heliopolis; the Buchis bull was the god Montu at Luxor. The ram was associated with the gods Amun and Khnum. Hathor was a cow, Anubis a jackal. Atum was a mongoose, Amun a goose. Sebek was a crocodile, Heket a frog, and Taweret a hippopotamus. Mafdet was a leopard or cheetah, Sekhmet a lion, Pahket ("she who scratches") a lioness, and Bastet a cat. Horus was a falcon, Thoth an ibis (or a baboon). The scarab beetle (a type of dung beetle) symbolized the god Khepri and was associated with the sun and movement.

Vast cemeteries of animal mummies, most dating to the Late Period and the Ptolemaic era, highlight the popularity of animal cults. Millions of cats, bulls, ibises, and crocodiles were mummified and buried with great ceremony. A 2003 exhibit in Cairo included two gilded limestone shrew sarcophagi—topped with tiny golden shrews.

Late Period animal cults brought out an intolerance previously unknown in Egypt. Killing a cult animal, even by accident, often brought heavy penalties—even death.

(much smaller and steeper than those at Giza) in their homeland.

When the Nubian pharaoh Taharqa meddled in Palestine, though, it angered the Assyrians, a powerful empire in the Near East that had control of the region. During a half-century of power struggles and open warfare, the Assyrians sacked Memphis and Thebes, looting the fabulous treasuries of the Amun-Re temples. The Nubians were driven back to their historical borders south of the first cataract. Thereafter, their contacts with Egypt were limited to trade.

The Twenty-sixth Dynasty

Aided by Greek mercenaries, Psamtik I of Sais took the throne, founding the Twenty-sixth Dynasty. For the next 139 years, the Saites presided over a relatively orderly, prosperous Egypt, consisting of (according to Herodotus) more than 20,000 towns. They used a combination of force and diplomacy to reunite Upper and Lower Egypt. They hired Greek mercenaries for the army, and oversaw the development of Egyptian naval power. The Assyrians had their own problems and left Egypt alone. Most of Egypt's eastern allies were being conquered by the Persian king Cyrus the Great.

The Saites carried on a vast trade around the Mediterranean. King Necho II preceded the modern Suez Canal (connecting the

Mediterranean and Red Seas) by 2,500 years by building a canal connecting the Nile to the Red Sea. They welcomed foreign traders, building towns where foreigners could live as national communities. They allowed the Greeks to colonize Naukratis in the Delta as a "free trade zone," where Greek traders enjoyed many privileges and rights.

The Saite Dynasty was an era of nostalgia. Saite kings revived ancient religious, artistic, and cultural traditions. They resurrected the Pyramid and Coffin Texts (see page 95). They built tombs at Giza and Saqqara, to be near the ancient kings. Animal cults became extremely popular.

The Saite kings were well aware of the wealth and power of the Theban priests of Amun-Re, and of their history of proclaiming themselves kings. To secure their power over these powerful priests, the Saite kings revived a New Kingdom custom of naming the king's eldest daughter God's Wife of Amun. The old title had been largely honorary, but the new one packed real power. The princess lived at the temple of Amun-Re at Karnak. Revered as a near-goddess, she performed religious rituals and controlled vast wealth and great estates. She was not allowed to marry, but

Sacred Insect
The scarab beetle symbolized the god Khepri, who was associated with the sun and movement. This scarab, carved with hieroglyphics on the underside, is made of green stone and gold. It dates from around 1200 B.C.E.

Nubian King
Granite sphinx of the Nubian pharaoh Taharqa. The Nubians, who had long been vassals of Egypt, became its rulers during the Twenty-fifth Dynasty.

she could adopt an heir. Holding this post gave the king's daughter enormous personal wealth, power, and influence—and kept the throne safer for her father, because the Amun-Re priests all answered to her.

But once again, winds of change were blowing around the Mediterranean. The Babylonian Empire came to regard Egypt as its enemy. Babylon defeated Egyptian forces in the Near East and seized Egypt's foreign territories. Then, the Persian king Cyrus the Great conquered the Babylonians. In 525 B.C.E., the inexperienced king Psamtik III faced the Persian army of Cambyses at Pelusium on the eastern frontier. Defeated, he fled back to Memphis, but was hauled off in chains to the Persian capital. The Twenty-sixth Dynasty collapsed in confusion.

Sunset of Native Rule

Cambyses had a reputation as a cruel tyrant. Fortunately, he only ruled Egypt for three years. He was followed by Darius I, a kinder, gentler Persian. Darius supported Egyptian animal cults and added to temples. He also improved the canal between the Nile and the Red Sea.

Still, the Egyptians were extremely unhappy about being part of somebody else's empire. Xerxes, another tyrant, put down several Egyptian rebellions. After 120 years, the Egyptians threw off Persian rule, regaining their independence for 67 years.

The Twenty-eighth Dynasty had only one, obscure, king, Amyrtaeos, who ruled for 10 years. Chaos in the Twenty-ninth Dynasty left a power vacuum. A usurper, Hakor, seized the throne. Ruling for 12 to 19 years, Hakor completed many building and refurbishing projects. Aided by Greek mercenaries, he turned back a series of Persian attacks.

The Thirtieth Dynasty beat back an attack by combined Persian and Greek forces. Nakhtnebef I (Nectanebo I) enjoyed a stable, 19-year reign, restoring temples all over Egypt. The 19-year reign of Nakhthoreb (Nectanebo II) saw a return to stability, the old gods, and traditional values. But Nakhthoreb was the last native Egyptian to rule Egypt for 2,300 years, until General Mohammed Naguib in 1952.

In 343 B.C.E., Persian ruler Ataxerxes reconquered Egypt. He drafted Egyptian sculptors and artisans to decorate palaces at the Persian capital, Persepolis. Again, the Egyptians chafed under foreign rule, and longed for rescue.

In 332 B.C.E., Mazaeus, governor (the office was known as *satrap*) under the Persian Darius III, opened the gates of Egypt to Alexander the Great, saving the country and his own life. Egypt welcomed Alexander as its savior—despite the fact that Alexander was Macedonian.

Egypt's Greek merchant community had long conducted wide-ranging, prosperous trade from their base at Naukratis in the Delta. Greek mercenaries, rising through the ranks, had modernized the Egyptian army and introduced new strategies and tactics. By the time of Alexander's arrival, old Egyptian traditions were already giving way to Greek culture.

Alexander, son of Philip of Macedon, was a brilliant military leader who set out to conquer the world. He swiftly conquered the entire Persian Empire. He was an enlightened ruler, often leaving conquered lands better off than they had been before his arrival. He used common social and economic concerns to unite diverse cultures and religions. At the same time, he established new cities to spread Greek culture.

Alexander, at 24, was already master of an empire when he reached Egypt. His first stop was the Oracle of Amun, who proclaimed him Amun's son and Egypt's rightful king, founding the Thirty-second Dynasty. Alexander was crowned pharaoh at Memphis with traditional religious splendor. He paid tribute to Egyptian gods and goddesses, repairing and restoring many temples, including Luxor. Alexander spent six months in Egypt setting up his new government. He appointed a viceroy and six governors. He converted Egyptian finance, tax, and bureaucratic systems to follow Greek models. He founded the new city of Alexandria, located on the coast at the Nile's west mouth—the ideal spot for it to become the commercial hub for the entire eastern Mediterranean. This Greek city became Egypt's new capital and a center of Greek learning and culture.

Alexander left troops stationed at Memphis and at Pelusium on the eastern frontier, put his own officers in charge of the Nile fleet, and left to conquer the rest of the world. But he became ill and died in 323 B.C.E. Alexander's empire was divided among his top generals. Ptolemy, one of the most trusted of his generals, got Egypt. For a time, Alexander's half-brother and then his son were the rulers of Egypt in name, although Ptolemy was actually in charge. Then, in 305 B.C.E., he was crowned Ptolemy I—the beginning of the Thirty-second (Ptolemaic) Dynasty.

Ptolemy's first move was to "kidnap" Alexander's body as it passed through Egypt on its way to Greece for burial. Alexander, whom the Egyptians considered a god, was buried at Alexandria. This gave Ptolemy tremendous religious and political clout. To further strengthen his position, Ptolemy married the daughter of Nectanebo II, the last native Egyptian king.

Under the Ptolemies, Egypt looked outward to Greece, not inward into the Nile Valley. The new upper class was Greek. The rulers paid lip service to Egyptian religion and traditions—they appeared in paintings and statues with Egyptian royal dress and symbols—but to the outside world they were Greek rulers, appearing on coins in Greek dress and trappings.

The Ptolemies were patrons of the arts. They expanded and supported the Library at Alexandria,

CONNECTIONS >>>>>>>>>>>>>

Mapmaking and Cartography

For half a century (247 B.C.E.–195 B.C.E.), the Greek scientist and geographer Eratosthenes was keeper of the great Library at Alexandria, home to thousands of ancient Egyptian documents recorded on papyrus scrolls. He took advantage of the opportunity to examine centuries of Egyptian land use records, carefully recorded by generations of scribes.

Very early in their history, the Egyptians had developed sophisticated techniques for accurately measuring large tracts of land. This was necessary to reestablish property boundaries after the annual inundation. These techniques, evolved and improved upon over time, eventually formed the basis for the maps Eratosthenes used to calculate the length of a degree of latitude, one of the cornerstones of modern cartography (mapmaking).

attracting scholars from all over the world. Temples they built at Dendera, Edfu, Philae, Esna, and Kom Ombo still draw tourists today. They built many new cities and towns. The Pharos of Alexandria, an immense lighthouse that was one of the seven wonders of the ancient world, was completed by Ptolemy II.

Under the Ptolemies, Egypt was prosperous and stable, exporting huge quantities of papyrus and grain all over the Mediterranean. But as a family, the dysfunctional Ptolemies were united mainly by shared names and bad behavior. The Ptolemies were fond of high living and gross excess; Ptolemy X was so fat that he could not walk unaided.

The Ptolemaic court was a complex, ongoing soap opera of scheming courtiers, corrupt officials, double-crossing advisors, and backstabbing siblings. It was peppered with intrigue, conspiracies, rivalries, and murders. It is difficult to sort out the players. All the kings were named Ptolemy, and most of the royal women were named Cleopatra, Berenice, or Arsinoe. At least two Ptolemies married their sisters named Arsinoe. Other Ptolemies also married their sisters, claiming reverence for Osiris and his sister-wife, Isis. But their motives were usually political, not religious.

By the time of Ptolemy VII, Rome was the Mediterranean's dominant power. Like bickering children, feuding Ptolemies ran to Rome for help. Ptolemy XII paid a large bribe (with Egyptian government funds) to Roman emperor Julius Caesar to be backed as king. Rulers around the region took advantage of Egypt's internal disorder to seize her possessions and naval bases. Egypt became a rich pawn in Roman power struggles—vital because Egyptian grain fed the Roman mobs.

The last Ptolemy, Cleopatra VII, became queen at age 17. A talented, ambitious woman, she is said to be the only one of the Ptolemies who could understand and speak Egyptian. Her older brother, whom she was scheduled to marry, tried to kill her instead (this was typical Ptolemaic behavior). She fled to Rome—and returned with an army. Julius Caesar favored her claim, and her. Cleopatra became Caesar's mistress and they had a son. She then married her younger brother, who became king.

After the death of Julius Caesar, Cleopatra took up with Mark Antony, a former Roman consul who was engaged in a power struggle with Caesar's heir, Octavian (the future emperor Augustus Caesar). The Battle of Actium, off the coast of Greece in September, 31 B.C.E., left Octavian victorious. In August, 30 B.C.E., Octavian entered Egypt, claiming it for Rome. Rather than surrender, Cleopatra committed suicide. Dynastic Egypt died with her.

CONNECTIONS >>>>>>>>>>>>>>>>>>>>>>>>>>>>>>>>>>>>

The Birth of Scientific Medicine

Early Greek physicians and scientists had a great curiosity about human anatomy and the inner workings of the human body. But Greek religious and cultural traditions did not permit them to systematically dissect corpses. So they traveled to Egypt in order to observe mummifications.

Egyptian physician-priests had been mummifying human bodies for thousands of years. But because they looked at corpses through religious, not scientific, eyes, they still had very little knowledge about human anatomy. Their goal was to preserve the body, not to understand it. In a short time, visiting Greek physi-

cians learned more about the structure and workings of the human body than Egyptian physician-priests had learned in millennia.

At the same time, the visiting Greeks took careful note of the more practical and effective treatments offered by Egyptian physicians: setting broken bones, the use of bandages, compresses and splints for injuries, simple surgeries, and potions and prescriptions that actually worked. These Greek observations of Egyptian medical knowledge—and their ability to separate the merely magical from the reliable and scientific—helped form the basis of Western scientific medicine.

Octavian ran Egypt as his personal estate, selling Egyptian grain to feed the Romans' endless appetite for "bread and circuses"–free food and entertainment supplied by the government. Roman Egypt was extremely prosperous and productive, and the population grew rapidly. Several Roman emperors appear in Egyptian trappings on monuments within Egypt, but it was just a political fiction.

Major changes lay ahead. The spread of Christianity wiped out most traces of the old Egyptian religion. The Coptic language evolved from earlier Egyptian. Hieroglyphics, hieratic, and demotic writing disappeared, replaced by the Greek alphabet with a few additional letters. The last known hieroglyphic inscription was carved on a temple at Philae in 394.

Egypt remained a territory of the Roman Empire, and then the Byzantine Empire, until Arab general Amr ibn el-As conquered the area in 641. The Arabs introduced the Islamic faith to Egypt. Although a small, strong Christian community survived (they became known as Coptic Christians), Egypt became, and remains, an Islamic nation, firmly a part of the Arab cultural tradition.

PART II

SOCIETY AND CULTURE

Egyptian Society

Everyday Life in Egypt

Egyptian Religion, Science, and Culture

CHAPTER 4

Egyptian Society

THE EGYPTIANS WERE PRACTICAL, TRADITION-LOVING, conservative, orderly, and tolerant. They organized the world into categories, with clear outlines and defined boundaries. They were suspicious of the unknown and avoided unnecessary risks. Their government was highly centralized and heavily bureaucratic. They were dedicated record keepers. They loved peace and order, and had little instinct for warfare. They were inclined to live and let live.

Although much of what we know about the ancient Egyptians comes from tombs, temples, and mummies, they were not a people obsessed with death. They loved the elements of their good life—festivals, music, color, ornament, beer, wine, and sweets—and simply wanted to make sure they could also have these things in the afterlife.

The Nile Valley is a long corridor linking Africa with the Near East. The Egyptians reflected ethnic influences from both regions. Some had dark skin and features typical of the peoples of central Africa. Others were lighter or olive-skinned, with Mediterranean or Near Eastern features.

They had no notion of "race" based on skin color or appearance. Since the earliest days when the region was settled, easy travel up and down the Nile ensured that people from different regions and with different ethnic backgrounds mixed and intermarried. Travelers and invaders also intermarried and intermingled with the local people.

The Egyptians did make one major distinction: There were the people of Kemet, who spoke the Egyptian language and followed Egyptian religion and customs ("us"); and the people who did not ("them"), considered misguided and inferior.

Always a Party

With more than 2,000 gods and goddesses, there was always an excuse for a festival. Some festivals lasted weeks, attracting thousands of visitors. The historian Herodotus witnessed a festival honoring the cat-headed goddess, Bastet, at her sacred city, Bubastis, and wrote about it in *The Histories*, Book 2:

> [T]hey come in barges, men and women together, a great number in each boat; on the way some of the women keep up a continual clatter with castanets and some of the men play flutes while the rest, both men and women, sing and clap their hands....When they reach Bubastis they celebrate the festival with elaborate sacrifices and more wine is consumed than during all the rest of the year. The numbers that meet there are, according to native report, 700,000 men and women....

These wild religious festivals were also long holidays from work. Priests distributed food, beer, wine, and other luxuries. Then, as now, free food and drink were always welcome.

Divine Balance

The guiding principle of Egyptian society was *ma'at*, which means balance, rightness, order, justice, truth, harmony, good behavior, and the status quo. The stability and predictability of the Nile contributed to this world view.

In nature, *ma'at* was the rising and setting of the sun, the orderly progression of the seasons, and the annual inundation. In daily life and business, *ma'at* was fairness and justice. In government affairs, *ma'at* meant the status quo: following traditions and precedents and not rocking the boat. In religious matters, *ma'at* meant living a good life, honoring the gods and goddesses, and being tolerant. Everyone, even the king, was expected to live by *ma'at*.

Ma'at was also the name of the goddess of balance and order. She, and the idea of *ma'at*, were sometimes associated with the cat (*mit* or *miit*), because of the balance between fierceness and gentleness the Egyptians saw in cats.

The opposite of *ma'at* was *isfet*—chaos, mischief, disruption, and disorder—represented by the god Seth. He was associated with the red lands of the desert.

Egyptian society was like a pyramid. At the top, set apart like the golden capstone on the Great Pyramid, was the king. At the broad base of the social pyramid were peasants, 80 percent of the population. In between were priests, government officials, artisans, tradesmen, and soldiers.

Egyptian society consisted of a wealthy, privileged elite, masses of very poor peasants, and (after the Middle Kingdom) a small middle class of artisans and professionals. The wealthiest families enjoyed diets, clothing, possessions, lifestyles, pleasures, and conveniences that the poorest could not even imagine. Yet even the poorest Egyptians had advantages not dreamed of by peasants in other parts of the ancient world. Compared to other ancient lands, Egypt was lucky, healthy, and prosperous.

The King and His Palace

At the top of the pyramid were Egypt's kings, who were also viewed as gods. They were responsible for the country's spiritual and material well-being. As the living embodiment of the god Horus, the king battled cosmic forces, upholding *ma'at* against *isfet*. As chief priest and fertility symbol, the king was responsible for the prosperity of the land, the success of crops, the annual, moderate inundation of the Nile, and the daily rising and setting of the sun. As military leader, he had to keep Upper and Lower Egypt united and content, and protect Egypt from enemies and invaders.

He was chief rainmaker and water-finder. His coronation took place at the beginning of *akhet*, the inundation season, to symbolize his power over the river. He was Egypt's role model for proper behavior and

CONNECTIONS >>>>>>>>>>>>>>>>>>>>>>>>>>>>>>

The Balance Beam Scale

As early as 1350 B.C.E., the Egyptians had developed accurate balance beam scales that could weigh small quantities of materials with an accuracy of plus or minus 1 percent. These scales were substantially similar to the balance beam scales used in modern chemical laboratories until quite recently (when they were largely replaced by even more accurate digital scales). Mechanical balance beam scales are still widely used in commerce and in everyday applications that do not require minute accuracy.

Balance beam scales are simple in concept but very difficult to make highly accurate. A horizontal beam is pivoted at the center of a vertical post. Suspended from the ends of the beam are two platforms. One platform carries the object or material to be weighed. The other carries an object (or objects) of known weight. A wooden balance beam scale found in the ruins of Akhetaten (Amarna) came complete with a collection of small weights in the forms of birds and animals.

For the Egyptians, balance beam scales had deep religious significance as well as practical applications. After death, each person's heart (the seat of his or her soul) was weighed against the "feather of Ma'at" on the scales of Ma'at, the goddess of balance and order. Beautifully illustrated copies of the Book of the Dead (see page 95) clearly depict this dramatic scene, complete with Ma'at's balance beam scales.

ma'at. Everything he said was law. Justice in Egypt meant "what the king loves"; wrongdoing was "what the king hates."

The king owned everything (symbolically, if not in practice)—all land, resources, animals, crops, people, every ounce of gold, every jar of beer, and every mud-brick in every peasant's hut. He held absolute power over life and death. Everything the king touched—his clothing, crowns, jewelry, tools, food, sandals, beer mug—was blessed with magic rituals and reserved for his use alone. Much of his time was spent performing magical and religious rituals to keep the universe running properly. His performance of these rituals magically activated similar rituals performed by lesser priests.

The palace, called *per-aa* (which means "great house"), was a complex of residences for the king and his family, harem, friends, personal staff, and government officials. It was also the seat of the central government and the military headquarters. It housed a major temple with its own priesthood. Many kings maintained two Great Houses (in Upper and Lower Egypt) and also many secondary palaces.

The Great House was a place of luxury, splendor, and ceremony. No effort or expense was spared to impress visitors. Everything the king did followed strict protocol. He was constantly surrounded by officials, priests, courtiers, visitors, and favor-seekers. He enjoyed the best of everything—except leisure and privacy.

Numerous favorites and officers of the court and their families and staffs lived at court at the king's expense. These Honored Ones, as they were known, were granted special favors: tombs near the king's, and lavish grave goods (linen, oils, wood for coffins, stone for sarcophagi). In the Old Kingdom, these honors meant they would join the king in eternal life—an extremely rare privilege.

Highest in status were the posts of King's Friend and Unique Friend. Other prized posts were Lordship of the Secret of the Royal House (keeper of the crown jewels) and Lordship of the Secret of all the Royal Sayings (issuer of invitations into the king's presence). The Director of the King's Dress supervised a large staff, including the Valet of the Hands, Director of Oils and Unguents, Keeper of the King's Wigs, and Groom of the Bedchamber. Each supervised large staffs.

The king chose his heir from among his sons—usually the son of his chief wife. If he had no sons, the king might choose a senior official who had married a princess. Many princes were prepared for kingship, just in case (although some went into military or religious service, particularly if an heir emerged early on). They studied astronomy, mathematics, civil engineering, architecture, and magical-religious rituals and spells.

Princes participated in hunting expeditions, military tournaments, and sporting competitions. They were expected to show exceptional talent and ability. Some princes ruled as co-regents (co-kings) with their fathers, although the extent of co-regency is controversial among Egyptologists. Many princes apprenticed in the army and took part in military campaigns.

While still a child, the crown prince (the one selected to be heir to the throne) was generally married to a sister, half-sister, or cousin. This kept the royal bloodlines "pure" and honored the god Osiris and his sister-wife, the goddess Isis.

Royal Ladies and Harem Women

The king's mother (known as the "great royal mother") and the king's chief wife (known as the "great royal wife") were associated with the goddess Hathor, and enjoyed near-divine status. A few women reigned as kings, and others reigned as co-regents with underage relatives. Royal ladies had lavish funerals, tombs, and grave goods, though not as elaborate as those of kings. Princesses received some education, sometimes learning to read and write.

Wealthy and royal ladies managed multiple large estates and supervised hordes of servants. Especially during the imperial age, they enjoyed the best the world could offer. They anointed themselves with costly imported perfumes, sipped the finest wines and dined on exotic delicacies. They owned huge collections of wigs and jewels. Their clothing chests bulged with finery, from royal linen smocks so fine they were transparent, to pleated and embroidered gowns made especially for them.

Particularly during Egypt's imperial age, kings kept harems of hundreds of wives, many brought from foreign lands (along with their many servants and attendants) to cement diplomatic ties with distant parts of the empire. Talented female singers, dancers, and musicians were often added to the royal harem to entertain at court.

Although she was married to the king, a harem woman might seldom see him. Still, there was always a chance he might single her out as a favorite. And there was a small chance that the king's great wife would not bear a son, and the son of a harem woman would be promoted to crown prince. Whatever her origin, a woman whose son became king became a queen herself—the great royal mother.

THE KING'S SYMBOLS

The king's royal dress included many symbolic items.

- The double crown (sekhemty) combined the crowns of Upper and Lower Egypt.

- The false beard, woven of rushes, symbolized divinity. Even female kings wore it.

- A bull's tail attached to the back of his kilt gave the king magical protection from the rear.

- The sacred uraeus, a spitting cobra, circled the king's crown or headdress, symbolizing his role as protector of Egypt.

- The protective falcon (the god Horus) encircled his head or stood behind him.

- The shepherd's crook, carried in the left hand, symbolized the king's gentleness, persuasive powers, and love for his people.

- The flail (a small whip), carried in the right hand, symbolized the king's power to compel, showing that he was fierce, fearless, and all-powerful.

Nobles and Priests

A few hundred privileged families controlled most of Egypt's wealth. Wealth meant land ownership. The king (who owned everything) granted large estates to his relatives, friends, and favorites. These large landowners paid no taxes, but collected heavy taxes from their serfs (the peasants on their estates). They became fabulously wealthy "little kings." Nobles had a moral duty under *ma'at* to care for the less fortunate, but were not legally required to do so.

Priests performed daily religious-magical rituals for the dead, and for gods and goddesses. These elaborate rituals were based on ancient traditions and had to be carried out exactly the same way every time. If the king—Egypt's chief priest—did not perform the proper daily rituals, the rituals performed by ordinary priests were worthless.

The dead and the gods required daily nourishment. Rituals included offerings of food and drink, sacrifices of animals, and magical spells. One important ritual in every temple was the daily washing, feeding, and clothing of the statue of the god or goddess.

Individual priests had specialties such as teaching, record-keeping, caring for the dead, presiding at funerals, sacrificing animals, or caring for the god's statue. They paid no taxes and were supported by the government. All but the smallest temples included granaries, libraries, healing centers, and schools. Temples also employed staffs of artisans, craftsmen, scribes, butchers, bakers, herdsmen, cooks, guards, doorkeepers, and janitors.

In large temples dedicated to the major gods, priests controlled enormous wealth. At the height of their prosperity under Twentieth Dynasty king Ramesses II, the priests of Amun-Re at Thebes controlled 90,000 serfs, thousands of acres of farmland, 500,000 head of cattle, 400 orchards, 80 ships, and 50 workshops. The Amun-Re temples received all the revenues from 65 towns and cities in Egypt and its empire.

Most priests were part-timers, working at small temples of local gods or goddesses. As Egypt's most educated class, priests were physicians, undertakers, embalmers, astronomers, mathematicians, architects, librarians, teachers, and scribes. They also ran the temple schools.

While on duty, a priest had to be ritually pure. This meant shaving his head and body and cleaning his mouth with natron (a drying mineral), among other ritual practices. There were many things he was not allowed to do, and many things he was required to do. While performing rituals, priests wore leopard skins, masks, wands of office, and elaborate jewelry.

Women were not allowed to become priests. However, they could be professional mourners at funerals, reenacting the grief of the goddesses Isis and Nephthys at the death of Osiris. They could be sacred prostitutes in the temples of the fertility god Min, or temple musicians, shaking the sistrum (a sacred musical rattle) or playing instruments during ceremonies and processions. They also helped tend their families' funerary cults, bringing offerings to the dead or burning incense at tombs. The term "priestess" generally meant a temple prostitute or a musician.

Government Officials

The vizier, or *tjaty*, was the king's top government official. He was the king's eyes and ears, his right-hand man, his enforcer, and his chief advisor. Though the vizier enjoyed immense personal wealth, prestige, and power, he also carried heavy burdens of responsibility.

He consulted daily with the king about major issues and decisions. He planned the king's schedule, hired and fired royal household staff, and supervised the king's bodyguard. As manager of the state archives, he inspected and approved government documents, issued receipts from royal storehouses and granaries, and dispatched palace messengers and diplomats. As acting chief justice of the courts, he judged land disputes. He oversaw the cattle census. Every few months, he toured the country, inspecting canals, reservoirs, and dams. He supervised tree-felling and shipbuilding. He made sure the border fortresses were well-supplied and secure. He organized defenses and ordered counter-measures against border raids. No wonder Rekhmara, vizier of Eighteenth Dynasty king Thutmose III, was known to rise before dawn and wander the streets of Thebes.

The vizier supervised a personal staff of scribes, assistants, couriers, guards, and stewards. Many kings had two viziers—one for Upper and one for Lower Egypt. In the early dynasties, the vizier was usually a relative of the king. The job could be passed from father to son, but only in cases of ability and merit. Kings were advised to appoint only very rich men—who were less likely to be tempted by bribes—as viziers.

Some viziers were also architects, physicians, and astronomers. One of the most famous, Imhotep, was vizier to Third Dynasty king Djoser. Called "Egypt's Leonardo da Vinci" because he was master of so many subjects, Imhotep was a brilliant architect. He designed the first pyramid, Djoser's Step Pyramid. He was the first to do large-scale building entirely in stone. Imhotep was also famous as a physician, mathematician, astronomer, magician, statesman, and wise man. He was credited with inventing the calendar. In later years, he was worshiped as a god and was considered a son of Ptah, god of arts and learning.

Like modern bureaucrats, viziers loved to expand their departments. Reporting to the vizier were several sub-viziers, cabinet officers, and department heads. The chief steward, master of the horse, scribe of the recruits, and superintendent of works also reported to the vizier, as did the *nomarchs*–governors of Egypt's 42 districts (called *nomes*). The chancellor (known as director of the seal) oversaw taxes, trade, and economic affairs. Overseers of the treasury looked after raw materials, tribute, plunder, and commodities. Overseers of the granary managed harvesting and storage of crops.

Egypt's government was many-layered, bureaucratic, and very expensive to run. It collected heavy taxes and spent lavishly. Huge departments—in charge of farming, granaries, taxes, frontiers, trade, health, the army, shipbuilding, foreign diplomacy, law—had branch headquarters in Upper and Lower Egypt. Each had many sub-departments and regional offices.

Regional officials stationed throughout Egypt and in conquered provinces reported to the vizier. One of the most powerful regional officials was the viceroy of Nubia. He ran conquered Nubia, oversaw military forces and border forts, and kept the southern trade routes open. He commanded a large bureaucracy and ruled independently, far from the king's eye. This job was usually passed from father to son.

Egypt was divided into 42 nomes (provinces): 22 in Upper Egypt, 20 in Lower Egypt. Throughout Egypt's history, the nomes were the basic administrative units of government. Nome boundaries were ancient, and *nomarchs* were descendants of Predynastic tribal chieftains. The *nomarch* was governor, chief judge, and high priest of the local god or goddess. Each town or city had a Council of Elders that reported to the *nomarch*.

The Middle Class

Among the middle class that emerged during the Middle Kingdom were independent artisans, tradesmen, scribes, and professional soldiers. Most lived in towns or cities, in districts with other members of their profession. They formed informal guilds and tradesmen's groups. They did not own land, but often had considerable personal wealth and many possessions. They were dependent on wealthy customers and clients, but were not tied to a wealthy landowner's estate the way the mass of peasants were.

Only 2 to 5 percent of Egyptians could read and write. They were scribes, essential to Egypt's diverse agricultural economy and bureaucratic government. When a government official visited an outlying district to inspect granaries, enforce tax collections, hold a criminal trial, open a new temple, supervise repair of a dam or canal, or oversee a building project, a team of scribes was there, writing everything down.

Like modern technology workers, scribes traveled frequently for their jobs. Their equipment had to be as compact, lightweight, portable, and versatile as a modern business traveler's laptop and personal organizer. A scribe carried his tools in a custom-made box decorated with colorful designs. He had a small palette (like a child's watercolor box) with shallow pots of dry red and black ink. (He often carried blue, green, and yellow ink, too.) He packed small pots for gum (a binder for ink) and water, a mortar and pestle for grinding ink, lumps of raw pigments, extra pens and papyri, brushes made of rope or crushed twigs, tools for repairing his pens and brushes, and a clipboard-like writing surface. He was ready for any job.

Ready to Write
This Eighteenth Dynasty stone relief shows scribes with their pens and papyrus ready.

The scribe moistened his reed pen in gum and drew it across one of the colors on his palette. In flowing hieratic script, he wrote on papyrus propped up on his writing surface. Many statues depict the typical posture of a scribe, sitting cross-legged, looking up alertly, pen raised, ready to write.

Scribes were always in demand and always busy. Scribes were the glue that held Egypt together. A talented, ambitious scribe had his choice of interesting jobs. He could work in the royal household, on the vizier's staff, with a professional guild, or at the estate of a nobleman. He might work at a building site tracking labor, materials, and progress. He could work in a temple, copying religious texts, or teaching student scribes. He could provide sketches of hieroglyphic texts to stone carvers and painters working on decorating a tomb or temple.

Egypt's professionals—engineers, architects, astronomers, mathematicians, and physicians—came from the ranks of scribes. Scribes could become civil engineers, in charge of harbors, irrigation systems, roads, canals, and public works. They might accompany trading or mining expeditions to Nubia, Lebanon, or Sinai to negotiate trades, record transactions, or carry out surveying tasks. They might join diplomatic missions to document treaties and trade agreements.

Scribes were almost always men. The job was often passed down from father to son, but a clever peasant boy might be selected to attend a temple school. A Middle Kingdom literary work called *Satire of the Trades* impressed upon students the advantages of being a scribe, and the miseries of every other occupation.

Random Access

The Egyptians were fanatical record-keepers. They produced millions of papyrus documents. Only a tiny, random selection has survived, mostly by chance. Papyrus is durable, but was never meant to last thousands of years. The papyrus records that survived were preserved by the hot, dry climate in airless tombs, or were stored in sealed clay jars. Grave robbers ignored papyri, or tossed them into trash heaps.

Many papyri that survived unharmed until the 1800s were damaged or destroyed by early explorers, who did not realize how fragile or valuable they were. Adventurers tore apart tombs looking for gold and treasure. Papyri could not be sold, so they were tossed aside. Papyrus often crumbles to pieces when exposed to air and moisture, so many ancient records vanished soon after they were uncovered. Others were lost in transit or damaged by rough handling. Only a few early explorers recognized the historical value of these papyrus documents.

Modern scholars, called *papyrologists*, piece together and study the surviving papyri. They treasure every scrap of information from these rare, random records. Egyptian scribes would be amazed to find their wine sales receipts and cattle counts, their tallies of beer jars and grain harvests, their inventory lists and memos, their notes from boring diplomatic meetings, preserved as treasures in libraries and museums.

Scribes generally did not pay taxes. They were supported generously by the government and by temples. They were fed, housed, and given fine clothes. They performed no heavy labor. A scribe was sometimes his own boss (although most were part of a hierarchy of administration), and often supervised important projects. He was honored and respected by all, held up as a role model for the young. The scribe's exalted status also brought responsibilities. He was expected to be a man of uncommonly good character and to live up to the reputation of his profession. Scribes were held in such high esteem that wealthy men who were not scribes often had statues made depicting themselves as scribes.

Another way to raise one's status was in the military. Before the Middle Kingdom, Egypt did not have a standing army. Military forces had been drafted as needed, with each nome sending a quota of men. Military leaders were citizen soldiers, not professionals.

During Egypt's imperial age, however, military service became a profitable career. Professional officers were rewarded with tax-free estates, livestock, serfs, gold, ceremonial weapons, and comfortable retirement jobs.

During the New Kingdom, Egypt maintained two large armies in four divisions, stationed permanently in Upper and Lower Egypt. The army included infantry, scouts, charioteers, marines, and archers. Officers successfully used strategies, tactics, and innovations introduced by the Hyksos, including horses and chariots.

New Kingdom soldiers were a privileged, prosperous class. During peacetime, they lived in military communities. Soldiers returning from campaigns were rewarded with land, livestock, and serfs, which they could keep as long as at least one member of their family remained on active duty.

A military career was one of the few paths to status and wealth for a poor young man. Even common soldiers shared in battle plunder: cattle, weapons, and other loot taken from defeated peoples. Ahmes Penekhbet, a soldier who distinguished himself in battle against the Hyksos and Asiatics, won armlets, bangles, rings, two golden axes, and two silver axes. He also received the "gold of valor"—six gold flies and three gold lions—from the king.

Most Egyptians were unwilling to go abroad for military expeditions. They were terrified that if they died outside Egypt, their bodies would not be properly mummified or buried, the proper prayers and spells would not be said at their funerals (if they even had funerals), and they would lose their chance at eternal life. So even at the height of empire, much of the army was composed of mercenaries (soldiers for hire) and troops from conquered lands, especially Nubians. Late Period armies were manned heavily by Asiatics and Greeks. Slaves and foreign captives often won their freedom by joining the army.

Egyptian artisans, another part of the middle class, created beautiful work, but not for personal artistic expression. Their statues, paintings, and carvings had specific religious, magical, or ritual purposes. In the early days, art primarily served the dead (especially kings), and the gods. As Egypt prospered, the skills artisans had developed and refined were turned toward creating beautiful and useful objects for the living.

Most artisans labored anonymously in workshops as members of efficient production teams. Their work was dedicated to the glory of the king, the dead, and the gods and goddesses. They had plenty of opportunity to demonstrate technical excellence and pride in their

Student scribes practiced their skills by copying texts their teachers thought were inspiring or educational: religious works, magic spells, popular legends, and proverbs. Papyrus was too valuable to use as "scrap paper," so beginners copied their lessons on *ostraca*, flat flakes of limestone or broken pieces of pottery left over from building projects. Schoolboys also wrote graffiti and made drawings on *ostraca*. These *ostraca* were tossed into trash heaps after school. Archaeologists love ancient trash heaps. Scholars consider these *ostraca* among the most valuable records of Egypt. There are many religious documents and literary works that are preserved only on schoolboy *ostraca*. Those long-ago students would probably be surprised to find their ancient homework, graffiti, and rude drawings displayed in museums.

workmanship. Their work required talent, skill, patience, and discipline. Though it had to follow strict conventions and traditions, it was frequently witty and inventive, and almost always graceful and elegant.

Artisans apprenticed for years in workshops of master craftsmen. Most artisans did not know how to read or write. They copied plans and sketches provided by scribes or priests. While excavating the ruins of Akhetaten, king Akhenaten's short-lived capital at Tell el-Amarna, archaeologists discovered the remains of the workshop of the sculptor Thutmose. Buried under rubble and sand in his storeroom, they discovered several incomplete sculptures and models that Thutmose had probably used in training his apprentices.

One of these models was a painted limestone bust of Nefertiti, Akhenaten's queen (on page 62). Now displayed in the Egyptian Museum in Berlin, Germany, it has become one of the most treasured icons of ancient Egypt. Because of that bust, and because his workshop had been abandoned quickly and remained undisturbed for thousands of years, modern scholars know more about the life of Thutmose the sculptor than they do about many of Egypt's kings.

Another workers' colony, at Deir el-Medina near Thebes, was occupied by generations of artisans and tradesmen who worked on tombs in the Valley of the Kings. They lived with their families in a walled village, enjoying a large measure of independence and self-government. They worked four hours in the morning, took a lunch-and-nap break, then worked another four hours. They enjoyed one day of rest every 10 days (an Egyptian week). They took frequent time off for festivals and religious holidays. In their off hours, they were free to cut and decorate tombs for themselves and their families in the nearby cliffs. Some worked part-time as priests.

They were paid in wheat and barley. The government supplied rations of fish, vegetables, oils, butter, salt, charcoal, wine and beer. They had servants to do laundry, haul water, grind grain, and catch fish. They employed cooks, butchers, rope-makers, weavers, and basket makers.

Serfs, Slaves, and Guards

Egyptian peasants were serfs, bound to their masters' land. They could also own their own land and animals. But most peasants owned very little, and everything they produced was heavily taxed. Most lived in small mud-brick houses in villages adjoining the fields. Each village had a Council of Elders, members of the principal families who handled day-to-day matters and minor disputes.

A peasant's life was one of constant, backbreaking manual labor. He planted, tended, and harvested his master's main crop. He labored in his master's garden, and tended his master's herds, flocks, and beehives. He carried endless heavy clay jars of water, balanced in pairs on a yoke across his shoulders, from river or canal to field and garden.

He drained marshes, removed wind-blown sand from fields, turned over soil, and planted, harvested, and cultivated vines and vegetable crops. Each year after the floodwaters receded, he helped local officials reestablish field boundaries and replace markers.

He also put in regular duty on local projects: digging and clearing canals, repairing dikes and dams, and building and repairing roads. In his spare time, he could work in his own garden and tend his animals.

During the inundation, the fields were under water and most peasants had nothing to do. The government took advantage of this idle labor force, drafting conscripts to construct royal tombs, build and enlarge temples, cut and haul stone, work mines, or for military campaigns.

Draftees had their heads shaved, said quick good-byes to their families, and boarded boats bound for job sites. They were assigned to crews and put to work. After the inundation was over, they usually returned home. Conscripts were not paid, either in money or in goods. This was

Who Is Winning?

Ancient papyrus doodles and graffiti, such as this lion and antelope playing a popular Egyptian board game, were tossed onto trash heaps in their day but are valuable artifacts in ours. This one is in the British Museum.

75

forced labor, but it was not slavery. The work was often brutally hard and dangerous, but conscripts were fed, housed, and treated reasonably well. Evading the labor conscript was a serious offense, punished harshly. One document calls for a punishment of 200 lashes and five open wounds. If a conscript deserted, his family might be imprisoned or held hostage until he returned. Conscripts who could afford to do so often hired a replacement worker—a practice that was tolerated, if not officially approved.

The government also used conscript labor to maintain irrigation systems. The canals, dams, dikes, and reservoirs that captured and managed the waters of the inundation were in constant need of enhancement, maintenance, and repair. Conscripts were put to work year round on these projects, and were sent wherever their labor was most needed.

Conscript labor was not popular, but many draftees probably saw their experience as an adventure. This might be their only chance to see the world beyond their village and participate in the great works of the age. A talented conscript might be noticed by an important official, and given education and training.

The concept of a slave as a person totally owned by another person did not exist. The line between "slave" and "citizen" was fuzzy. The personal slave of a wealthy man was often better off than a peasant. The slave could own property, and even have servants. He could purchase his freedom, or his master could free him with a word. Most Egyptian slaves were treated reasonably well, especially compared to slaves elsewhere in the world at the time. They were fed, housed, and given a yearly allocation of clothing, oils, and linen. When it was especially hot, their work hours were reduced.

Most slaves were foreign war captives from Asia or Nubia. They were considered ritually impure, and therefore could not enter temples or enjoy Egyptian burial rites. When they died, their corpses were thrown into the river for the crocodiles. In the Late Period, many for-

Onward Nubian Soldiers
A painted wood funerary model from an Eleventh Dynasty tomb, c.2000 B.C.E., shows a regiment of Nubian archers. Much of the Egyptian army was made up of foreign mercenaries, especially Nubians.

This Beer Is for Inty-shedu

In 1992, Dr. Zahi Hawass, secretary general of the Egyptian Supreme Council of Antiquities and director of the Giza Pyramids Excavation, was excavating a cemetery southeast of the Sphinx that includes more than 30 tombs of craftsmen and artisans who worked on the pyramids. One of these belonged to a carpenter and boat builder named Inty-shedu. The main burial shaft contained a skeleton and two jars of beer. Two other burial shafts held only skeletons.

Inty-shedu's tomb was a rare find in many ways, but held an extra surprise: a *serdab* with multiple statues. A *serdab* (Arabic for "cellar") is a wall niche or small chamber containing a miniature portrait statue of the deceased person. The *serdab* figure was a kind of insurance policy for the tomb owner: If anything happened to his mummy, his *ka* (spirit) would recognize the *serdab* figure, allowing him to still enjoy eternal life. The *serdab* statue was sealed into its chamber, with a tiny slot where the *ka* could enter.

Inty-shedu did not have the usual single statue, but five *serdab* figures depicting him at different ages. Like a modern man who wants the loudest stereo or the fastest car, Inty-shedu wanted to stand out from the afterlife crowd.

But he also wanted to be one of the guys. In his adult statues, Inty-shedu wears a sporty moustache. Archaeologists know that moustaches were popular among workingmen, while kings and nobles were generally clean-shaven.

Inty-shedu's portrait statues, crafted in painted limestone, are vivid and lifelike. It is easy to imagine "magically activating" one of them, opening a jar of beer and sitting down with Inty-shedu to talk about business at the boat yard.

eigners, including former slaves and descendants of slaves, rose to positions of power.

The Medjay (or Medjai) were desert wanderers from Nubia who were hired by Egypt as policemen, guards, and soldiers. The Medjay had reputations as fearless guards and brutal law enforcers. They punished criminals such as tax evaders and draft-dodgers, and guarded palaces, temples, and tombs all over Egypt. But no police force, even the fierce Medjay, was ever able to stop the robbers who looted just about every royal tomb in the land.

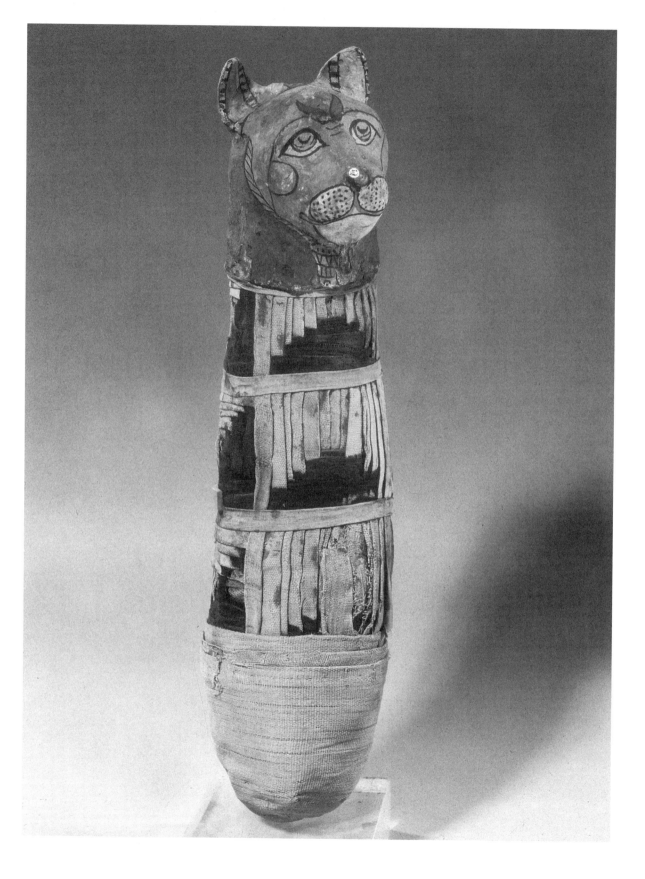

CHAPTER 5

Everyday Life in Egypt

AS EGYPT GREW AND PROSPERED, SOME OF THE SETTLEMENTS along the Nile blossomed into towns and cities, with districts for temples, tradesmen, artisans, and laborers. But most people lived in rural areas and villages. At most, 5 percent of the people were city dwellers. Walled or fortified towns, common elsewhere, were rare in Egypt. Cities and towns were hot, dry, and dusty, teeming with people and animals. Streets were cramped and narrow. Flies and biting insects swarmed and buzzed. Smoke from dung-fueled cooking fires hung heavily in the air.

Although clean in their homes and persons, the Egyptians, like other ancient peoples (and some modern ones), saw any space outside their front doors as a convenient dump. Trash and garbage were carted off to the nearest canal, thrown into alleys or temporary pits, or piled in heaps wherever there was space. Heated by the broiling sun, rubbish heaps quickly became noxious pest- and vermin-ridden nightmares.

Once the Egyptians domesticated the cat (during the Middle Kingdom), urban conditions improved. Cats quickly went to work killing rodents and other pests in alleys, dumps, homes, and granaries, improving health and preserving precious food supplies.

Homes and Other Buildings

Most homes and villages were set on high ground to protect them from the inundation. Settlements in low-lying areas were surrounded by dams and berms (a wall of earth) that required constant inspection and maintenance, lest water flood in.

Good-quality timber had to be imported, and building with stone was expensive and labor-intensive. Limestone, granite, massive wooden

OPPOSITE
Cats in Life and Afterlife
Mummified cats were common in Egyptian tombs because cats were so useful in life. By killing rodents and other pests, cats protected the food supply, kept the home cleaner, and enhanced family health. Millions of cats were mummified, and pilgrims to Bubastis, sacred city of the feline goddess Bastet, purchased cat mummies to leave as an offering.

pillars, and other expensive, durable materials were reserved for homes for the dead and homes for the gods.

Houses and other buildings for the living, from peasant's hut to king's palace, were built of mud-brick: clay-heavy mud from the Nile, mixed with chopped straw or sand and dried in the sun. By 3000 B.C.E., Egyptian builders were already expert mud-brick builders. They had even standardized brick sizes and shapes. The Egyptians knew how to fire bricks in a kiln. But sun drying was so easy and efficient, and made such strong, durable materials, they saw no need to go to the extra trouble. Sun-dried mud-brick was cheap, versatile, readily available, and could be worked quickly into structures of any size. In the hot, dry climate, mud-brick buildings lasted several generations.

Plumbing and Bathtubs

Most Egyptian homes lacked even primitive plumbing. Some middle- and upper-class homes had "earth closets": primitive toilets with limestone seats and a bucket of sand. Drainage went into sand layered beneath the house.

Some wealthy families had bathing rooms, which were recessed areas with limestone-slab floors. The bather stood in this "shower stall" while servants doused him with buckets of clean water. Drainage ran into a large earthenware bowl on the floor, or through a channel in the wall and out into a barrel outdoors. The practical Egyptians probably recycled the waste water into their gardens.

No one had running water. Water was carried, in large clay jugs and pots, from the nearest canal or the river. The backbreaking job of fetching a household's daily water supply was women's work. Some wealthy families had wells dug on their property, eliminating the need for constant water-hauling.

At one site, archaeologists found a stone bathtub with plastered sides and a drain. Water drained into a vase punched with holes and cemented into the earth. This bathtub was probably owned by a person who was so wealthy that he saw no need to conserve water.

Home for a peasant farmer or workman was just a few small rooms. At sites of major public projects, like the Giza plateau during the Fourth Dynasty pyramid age, the government built "workers' villages": rows or terraces of simple houses, much like the row houses in New England factory towns of the 1800s.

The typical home, humble or grand, followed a model still common in Egypt and other hot climates. To the street, the home presented a blank wall with a door. A visitor passed through a reception area before reaching a courtyard that was open to the sky.

Several rooms surrounded the courtyard. The most private ones were reserved for the women. The arrangement, size, number, furnishings, and decorations of rooms varied greatly, according to homeowner's wealth, status, and taste. Some homes had a second story or additional courtyards. Flat roofs accessed by staircases or ladders became breezy outdoor sleeping places on hot nights.

Thick walls of mud-brick helped keep interiors comfortable. Tiny windows set high in the walls helped heat escape. Some homes had small, triangular roof structures (called "wind towers") that funneled cooling north winds into the home. These were common features of Egyptian homes well into the 20th century. The few small openings were covered with linen hangings or wood shutters to help keep out dust and insects. Pots of scented oils sweetened the air.

Interiors were quite dark. They were lighted at night with small pottery oil lamps. (Herodotus found the scent of the Egyptians' castor oil lamps unpleasant.) Fancier homes were lit with elaborate lamps of carved translucent stone, such as alabaster. Most cooking was done in outdoor kitchens on stone hearths or metal braziers. The most common cooking fuel, still used in rural Egypt today, was cow dung. Charcoal and wood scraps were also occasionally burned.

Egyptians were fond of plants and flowers, and grew a great variety for home decoration, personal adornment, and offerings to the gods and the dead. Many herbs and flowers were used in food, cosmetics, and medicines. Country villas of wealthy families boasted lush gardens, irrigated year round with water carried in stone jars from a canal or the river. The courtyard was a pleasant retreat from the dirt, insects, and noise of the street. It might have a pool of cool water surrounded by flowering and vining plants, date palm and fig trees, and other fruit and shade trees. Some families planted sycamore trees, sacred to the goddess Hathor.

Many families plastered their interior walls and had them painted with colorful designs, flowers, animals, and nature scenes. Many homeowners laid floors of pressed clay or brick paving tiles, coated with smooth plaster. Floor coverings woven of reeds, papyrus, or palm straw helped trap the ever-present dust and sand, and served as sleeping mats.

Interior Decor

The Egyptians' clean, uncluttered interior decor would not look strange in an ultra-modern decorating magazine. Furnishings were few and simple: low tables, wood stools with woven rush seats, and stands or pedestals to hold platters of food. Chairs with arms were rare, and were reserved for important guests.

Most people slept on the floor on woven mats, although some used low, built-in platforms of brick or wood. According to Herodotus, people in Upper Egypt slept on raised platforms, above the clouds of flies and gnats, while in Lower Egypt, sleepers draped their mats with fine netting—which they used by day to catch fish.

During the prosperous New Kingdom, upper-class homes were more lavishly furnished, with beds, chairs, and couches topped with soft cushions. Furniture legs were carved in fanciful shapes, like animals' paws. Although their furnishings must have seemed luxurious to them, the homes of even the wealthiest Egyptians would look somewhat empty to modern eyes.

Mud-brick construction made it easy to build in handy wall niches for linens, pottery, and other household goods. Jewelry, linens, clothing, cosmetics, perfumes, toys, and other personal possessions were stored in wooden chests, boxes, or woven baskets.

The Egyptian Family and Household

The Egyptians highly valued marriage and family. The basic family unit was the nuclear family of father, mother, and children. Households often included unmarried or widowed female relatives, providing support for them and gaining extra hands for childcare and housework. Couples wanted as many healthy children as possible. If a married couple was unable to have children, they often divorced. Childless couples sometimes adopted children.

Women had a great deal of freedom, independence, and status under law and custom. Unlike women of most ancient societies, they could own or rent property, inherit wealth, own slaves, leave property to (or disinherit) their children, take legal cases to court on their own, operate businesses, work outside the home, and live alone without a male guardian. Their lives were not easy, though. Girls were married by age 12 to 14, as soon as they could have children. Many babies died in infancy, so it was important to make the most of a woman's fertile years.

Marriage was an agreement between a man and a woman to live together and have children. There was no official ceremony. Divorces, separations, and remarriages all occurred. Adultery was punished harshly, especially in women. Polygamy (a man taking multiple wives) was accepted, but in practice only wealthy men had multiple wives. Polygamy was too expensive for the average working man.

A married woman was called "mistress of the house." She was responsible for child care, cooking, hauling water, grinding grain, baking bread, brewing beer, spinning and weaving, making and repairing clothing, and tending the shrines of domestic gods and goddesses. Wealthy woman supervised many servants.

Pregnancy and childbirth were extremely dangerous for both mother and baby. Physicians could offer little help. Pregnant women recited magical spells and prayers, made offerings to Bes, Taweret, and Bastet, and wore protective charms and amulets. A woman gave birth in a squatting or kneeling position, balanced over a platform. A midwife stood by to help. Afterwards, the woman and her child had to leave home for several days for purification in a special "birth tent." Similar practices are still enforced in many societies around the world.

An Egyptian Child's World

A few Egyptians enjoyed long lives. Pepy II, last king of the Sixth Dynasty, ruled for more than 90 years. But most people did not live past 35 or 40. Three or four out of every five children did not survive to adulthood. A child who lived to celebrate his fifth birthday was lucky. Because so many children died young, children were only gradually included in the life of the family and community.

Childhood was brief but happy, with games, toys, and freedom. Egyptians often named (or nicknamed) their children after animals, such Monkey, Cat, Frog, Mouse, Hound, or Gazelle, based on the child's behavior. Miit (cat) was a popular name for girls.

Children played games much like today's: leap frog, running and jumping, swimming, tug-of-war, ball games of many kinds, and a form of hopscotch. Gymnastics, vaulting, and handball were popular with both boys and girls. One ancient game, "goose steps," is still played in rural Egypt. Girls played with dolls and small animal figurines. Children fished, swam, and rowed small boats. Some wealthy families had swimming pools.

Late childhood was devoted to preparations for adulthood. There was no such thing as a "teenager" as we know it. A peasant child's life of hard manual labor began early, helping with planting, harvesting, and threshing. Boys were considered fully adult by age 15 or 16. They were expected to take on adult responsibilities, adopt a profession, and support their families.

Girls almost never learned to read and write. Priests, nobles, and the wealthy sent their sons to temple schools to study under the strict guidance of priest-scribes. A peasant boy who showed extraordinary intelligence and promise might be sent to school—a major turning point in his family's fortunes, because the literate minority ran the country.

Most of a young man's higher education was on-the-job training, alongside a master in his chosen field. Youngsters studying to become priests, and students of mathematics, medicine, or astronomy, stayed at the temple school for advanced education.

Bread and Beer for Peasant and King

The staples (basic foods) for everyone, peasant to king, were bread and beer. Emmer and spelt, the two kinds of wheat grown in Egypt, were ground on a grinding stone called a *saddle quern*. This work was done by women, and was very hard on the back and knees. Bakers created dozens of kinds of bread, to be served with thick spreads of fava beans, lentils, or chickpeas.

Even humble homes had a kitchen brewery. To make beer, barley flour was formed into loaves, which were lightly baked. The baked loaves were soaked in tubs of water and allowed to ferment. Other varieties of beer were made from fermented wheat, wheat loaves, or plain ground, unbaked barley. Beer was sweetened with honey, dates, or fruit juices.

Wine made from fermented palm sap or grapes was also popular and widely available. Vineyards in the Delta produced the choicest wines, but several regions of Egypt and the western desert oases also produced distinctive vintages. Imported wines had snob appeal, just as they do today. Wealthy families grew grapes in their gardens and pressed their own wines. The Egyptians preferred their wine, like their beer, sweet, so they added honey or fruit juices. Beer and wine stayed cool in large, semi-porous, sealed earthenware jugs.

Even the poorest peasant could supplement his bread and beer with onions and eggs. Also on the regular menu was fish, caught in the Nile or in the many irrigation canals. Nile perch, catfish, and tilapia were spit-roasted over coals. Fish and pork were considered ritually impure, but both were common in peasants' diets.

Farm families kept flocks of fowl for the table. Goose, duck, crane, and pigeon, spit-roasted over glowing embers, were favorite menu choices and available to all but the poorest. Wild birds of the marshes were snared or trapped in nets, or brought down with boomerang-like throw-sticks. Some were killed and eaten; others kept in small flocks for eggs.

Wealthy families had a much richer and more varied diet. They regularly enjoyed milk, butter, and cheese from herds of cows and goats. They frequently ate beef, goat, lamb, and mutton (sheep), all rare in a peasant's diet. Nobles also dined on exotic meats such as gazelle and antelope.

A Wealth of Produce

Irrigated gardens around villas produced a bounty of fruits and vegetables: melons, figs, pomegranates, dates, onions, peas, chickpeas, beans, lentils, lettuces, leeks, cucumbers, cabbage, horseradish, spinach, turnips, carrots, eggplant, and radishes. Vines on trellises produced raisins, wine, and table grapes. Herb gardens featured dill, coriander, chicory, cumin, parsley, and various varieties of mint (possibly including catnip). Juniper berries were grown as a spice.

The Egyptians pressed oils from sesame seeds and castor beans for cooking, flavoring foods, and making medical and cosmetic potions. They pressed flax seeds for linseed oil. The most common oil was pressed from the fruit of the moringa tree.

Rich or poor, people ate with their fingers. In wealthy households, servants poured water over their masters' hands between courses and offered clean linen towels to dry them. Poor folks had to wash up all by themselves. Most households were well-equipped with earthenware jugs, pitchers, bowls, platters, and mugs. Wealthy families had sets of fancy

CONNECTIONS >>>>>>>>>>>>>>>>>>>>>>>>>>>>>>>>>

Marshmallows and Licorice

The Egyptians loved sweets: sweetened beer and wine, and marshmallows and licorice. Among the world's oldest sweets, marshmallow confections date back to 2000 B.C.E. Egyptians made a honey-based candy flavored and thickened with the sweet, sticky sap from the roots of the marshmallow (*Althaea officinalis*), a plant with hollyhock-like flowers that grew wild in salt marshes and in wetlands around the Nile. This special delicacy was said to be reserved for royalty, and for offerings to the gods. Until the mid-1800s, marshmallow candies still included many of the same ingredients the Egyptians used. In modern marshmallow recipes, gelatin or gum arabic replaces plant sap.

Egyptian physicians also used honey and the sap of the marshmallow plant in medicines and potions, especially in remedies such as medicinal wines used to treat sore throats—a practice common right through the 19th century.

Another plant the Egyptians both enjoyed as a sweet and in medical potions was licorice (*Glycyrrhiza glabra*). A supply of dried licorice root was found in Tutankhamun's tomb. The sweet root was chewed as a delicacy. Egyptian physicians also prescribed it to treat coughs and lung disease. Licorice root is still widely used as a flavoring and ingredient in foods and medicines. It is still grown in Egypt, and exported for use in organic foods, teas, and herbal medicines.

dishes made of fine alabaster, schist, or other decorative stone.

Until the New Kingdom, there were no dining room tables. Diners squatted on rush mats at low, multi-purpose tables, or stood up and plucked food from bowls or platters on stands, buffet style. The elite of the New Kingdom perched on high stools at large tables, or reclined on couches, while servants brought them food and drink.

Personal Appearances

Appearance, cleanliness, and good grooming were important. Even mummies were carefully manicured. Medical papyri include formulas for preventing baldness, fighting wrinkles, and coloring gray hair. The Egyptians washed with natron-and-oil soaps, shaved with copper or bronze razors, and plucked stray hairs with copper or silver tweezers. They applied eye paint (called kohl), scented oils, and deodorant made of powdered carob. They admired the results in hand-held mirrors of highly-polished copper.

Egyptian clothing was light, simple, and elegant, especially in the Old and Middle Kingdoms. Egypt was almost always hot, so both men and women wore as little as possible. Men wore plain linen loincloths that hung to the knees. Women wore linen shifts. Children generally ran about naked, wearing only amulets or charms (often depicting the god Bes) to protect them from harm.

The Height of Fashion
Long braided wigs were very fashionable among the wealthy women of ancient Egypt. The wigs were often reddened with henna and adorned with fresh flowers.

Many men shaved their heads—a sensible choice in a hot, dry, dusty, insect-infested land. Many women, including legendary beauty Nefertiti, did too. For dress-up, both men and women wore wigs made of human hair, or a mixture of hair and plant materials, stiffened with beeswax. Wigs came in many styles. Some included braids, plaits, ribbons, and jeweled ornaments. Wig fads came and went. Nefertiti favored a short, curly Nubian-style wig, widely copied by her subjects.

Children had shaved heads except for what was known as the "sidelock of youth" (also called the "Horus lock"), a narrow shock of hair left hanging to one side. The falcon-god Horus was the Egyptian archetype of the good son, and the Horus lock was worn as a pious reminder of Horus's role as a virtuous and devoted child. Cutting off of the side-lock was a rite of passage when a child became an adult.

During the New Kingdom, enormous wealth flowed into Egypt. The elite adopted colorful, elaborate clothing, jewelry, and personal adornments. Increased contact with the Near East, where colorful, ornamented textiles were popular, influenced fashions.

Women enjoyed the opportunity to dress up in elaborately pleated, embroidered, and decorated gowns, capes, and shawls in many colors. Even men got into the act, wearing richly pleated kilts, capes, and long skirt-like garments emblazoned with decorations and rich embroideries.

Even at their fanciest, Egyptian fashions were graceful, tasteful, and (almost) never overdone. Most clothing was made of natural-colored linen, spun and woven from flax, one of Egypt's major crops. Figurines and paintings show women in multi-hued sheaths with geometric patterns of red, yellow, and blue.

Egyptians went barefoot most of the time. During the prosperous years of the empire, royals and the elite completed their outfits with rush or papyrus sandals, leather shoes, or leather slippers. Both men and women wore clothing and accessories made of wool and leather. But these materials were not considered ritually pure, so leather and wool are seldom depicted in art works.

CONNECTIONS >>>>>>>>>>>>

Health, Beauty, and Tabby Cats

Men, women, and children of all ages and social groups wore heavy eye makeup called *kohl*. On stone palettes, they ground malachite (a green ore of copper) or galena (a dark gray ore of lead) into powder, blended it with fragrant oil, and applied it in thick bands above and below their eyes with a rounded-end tool called a kohl stick. They also brushed natural pigments made from colored earth and minerals onto their eyelids and eyebrows.

Scholars have long known that the thick eye paint offered some protection against the constant glare of the sun, blowing sand and dust, and the unavoidable clouds of insects. Eye paint was an ancient version of sunglasses; modern-day athletes still paint thick black lines under their eyes.

In 1999, Egyptologists and chemists studied the contents of several 4,000-year-old pots in the collection of the Louvre Museum in Paris, France. The pots were from ancient Egyptian makeup kits. The researchers found chemical compounds that were used thousands of years later by Greek and Roman doctors to treat infectious eye diseases such as conjunctivitis.

Elaborate eye paint was also a fashion statement, and even a form of religious devotion. Worshippers of the cat-headed goddess Bastet may have painted their eyes in imitation of the tabby markings on their cats' faces. The dark rings around a tabby cat's eyes are still called "eyeliner" today.

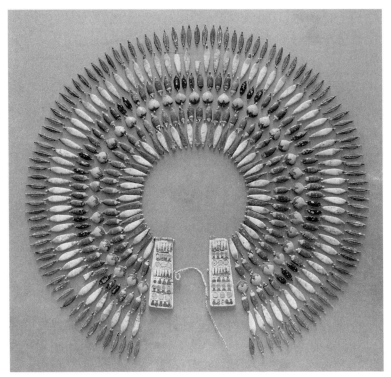

Fit for a King

Among the wealthy and royalty, elaborate jewelry was worn by both men and women. This neck collar, made of semiprecious stones, was found in the tomb of King Tutankhamun.

Jewelry and Amulets

Everyone wore jewelry. The wealthy had rich ornaments made of gold and decorated with amethyst, turquoise, lapis lazuli, and other gemstones. Less exalted folks wore strings or collars with faience beads and amulets (faience is pottery coated with brightly colored glazes). Jewelry, especially amulets and charms, had magical and protective powers. Carnelian, turquoise, and lapis lazuli brought luck. (These beliefs endure today, as the modern fashion of "power bead" bracelets.) Even the poorest peasant child wore a pottery or bone ring or amulet with a crude image of Bes.

Amulets magically attracted good luck and warded off evil. They protected the wearer from accidents, hunger and thirst, snakes, demons, and other everyday dangers. Amulets were made in many forms: scarabs and the *ankh* (symbols of eternal life), animals, gods and goddesses, crowns, and the Eye of Horus (symbol of wholeness).

The Egyptians and Animals

Most Nile Valley animals were not dangerous, and were easy to hunt, herd, or domesticate. Egyptians trusted amulets and magic spells to protect themselves from the exceptions: crocodiles, scorpions, and several kinds of snakes with deadly bites. When hippos were common, they caused much damage to crops and fields and were hunted as nuisances. Rats and mice that consumed and fouled stored grain were a huge problem until the cat was domesticated during the Middle Kingdom.

Hunting, fowling, and fishing in the marshes was a popular sport and a source of food. Subsistence hunting (hunting for daily food consumption) by large numbers of people became less important as farming and animal husbandry (raising domesticated animals) became widespread.

In Predynastic times, settlers rounded up the wild cows, bulls, oxen, gazelles, oryxes, and goats that roamed the Nile Valley into domestic and temple herds. Animals were raised for milk, hides, meat, and sacrifice to the gods. Geese, ducks, cranes, and pigeons were bred and fattened for food. The Egyptians practiced selective breeding to improve domestic animals.

Hunters speared and netted fish. They brought down game birds with boomerang-like throw sticks. They captured birds for domestic flocks, or to be fattened as religious sacrifices. Nobles and the wealthy continued to hunt for sport. They speared hippos and crocodiles. Royals and the elite enjoyed game drives in the marshes and desert edges, especially in the early years when there were still plenty of large animals. They took hippos, lions, leopards, antelopes, gazelles, ibexes, oryxes, giraffes, and elephants.

Like us, the Egyptians cherished pet dogs and cats as companion animals. From ancient times, dogs guarded herds and helped in game drives. Later Egyptians were great dog fanciers, breeding companion animals that looked much like modern Salukis. Dogs, usually depicted in the company of men, were named for their looks: Ebony or Big were common names.

Cats, who arrived in the Nile Valley during the Middle Kingdom, were originally prized for their ability to kill rodents and protect food supplies. But they were soon adopted as household pets. They not only controlled rats, mice, and snakes, but also offered companionship and pleasure. In Egyptian art, cats were usually shown with women.

After the Hyksos introduced horses, the Egyptians became famous horse breeders and charioteers. They did not ride the horses, however; scholars believe the spines of their horses were too weak to support riders.

Sports, Games, and Fun

Egyptians loved competition. The work gangs building the Great Pyramid engaged in rivalries, adopting team names and slogans, bragging about their own stone-hauling abilities, and taunting other crews for being lazy. Farmers harvesting crops lightened their burdens by choosing up sides and trying to outdo the other guys in cutting, threshing, and hauling.

CONNECTIONS >>>>>>>>>>>>>

Pack Animals

Pack animals may well have been in use for thousands of years by the time the Nile Valley was settled. But the first certain evidence of pack animals at work comes from Upper Egypt in the early dynastic era, around 3000 B.C.E.

Early settlers in the Nile Valley had tamed the donkeys that roamed the valley and gathered them into domestic herds. It probably was not long before a weary farmer or water carrier lashed his burden onto the back of one of these sturdy, uncomplaining beasts. By 2000 B.C.E., caravans of heavily-laden donkeys were common in Egypt, the Near East, and the surrounding deserts.

The king and wealthy nobles sponsored sporting events, providing equipment, announcing winners, and awarding prizes such as special collars. Players wore uniforms and shouted down the calls of supposedly neutral referees. Participants were cheered not only for winning, but for showing ability, grace, and good sportsmanship.

Older children and adults pursued athletic activities that resemble modern sports: handball, hockey, boxing and wrestling, long-distance running, weight lifting, long jump and vaulting, archery, javelin throw, sport fishing, and hunting. Drawings on tombs at Beni Hasan depict a sport much like hockey. Players wield bats made of palm branches, bent at the ends like hockey sticks. The ball was compressed papyrus fiber, covered in dyed leather. Rural Egyptians still play a similar game.

Egyptian team rowing resembled modern rowing sports. The leader, sitting at the rudder of the rowboat, called out high-pitched, rhythmic signals to synchronize the rowers and encourage them to greater speed. An ancient Egyptian rower, standing on the banks of the Charles River at Harvard University in Boston, Massachusetts, would instantly recognize his sport.

Long-distance running was a popular sport. It also had ritual significance for the king. As part of the *heb-sed* festival, held at intervals during each king's reign, the king ran a special course around the temple grounds. This ritual run confirmed that he was still physically and mentally fit to rule.

Egyptians enjoyed playing board games such as dog-and-jackal, *mehen* ("coiled serpent"), and *senet*. According to the Book of the Dead, they even played *senet* in the afterlife. Peter Piccione, professor of comparative ancient history at the College of Charleston in Charleston, South Carolina, thinks they played *senet* both for fun and for religious reasons. *Senet*, played with bone or ivory pieces on a board with 30 squares, enabled living players to communicate with the dead. When played in the afterlife, *senet* let the dead player's spirit move freely between heaven and earth. Four *senet* boards were found in Tutankhamun's tomb.

Music and Dancing

Music and dancing, originally part of religious rituals, quickly became popular in everyday life. The wealthy hired small orchestras and troupes of dancing girls to entertain at banquets. Musicians played wooden harps, flutes, pipes, clarinets, and trumpets. They clicked finger-clappers, shook the sistrum, and rattled their bead necklaces and other jewelry in time

GODSEND AND GODDESS

The Egyptian word for cat was *mit, miit, miw, miu,* or *mii*—"she who mews." The African wild cat (*Felis silvestris lybica*) was a godsend, and later a goddess, to Egypt. Cats were economically useful, religiously significant, and popular as pets.

Sometimes called "the gloved cat" for her distinctive forearm markings, the small, long-legged, sandy-colored mackerel tabby prized by the Egyptians is the ancestor of today's domestic cats. Genetic and anatomical research shows that all of today's domestic cats are descended primarily from *F. silvestris lybica*.

Take Me Out to the *Seker-Hemat*

The Egyptians were the first to play ball games. Egyptologist Peter Piccione, professor of comparative ancient history at the College of Charleston in Charleston, South Carolina, noticed a connection between an Egyptian religious ritual called *seker-hemat* ("batting the ball") and modern baseball, stickball, and softball.

He was studying wall paintings in a shrine of the goddess Hathor, at a temple built by Queen Hatshepsut at Deir el-Bahari. In one painting, Eighteenth Dynasty king Thutmose III holds a slender, bat-like stick in one hand and what looks like a baseball in the other. Two priests facing the king—catchers—hold similar balls.

Each night, as the sun traveled through the dangerous underworld, the serpent Apopi, who symbolized chaos, tried to devour it. The *seker-hemat* ball was the "eye of Apopi." By batting the ball, the king destroyed chaos, upheld *ma'at*, and made sure the sun rose in the morning.

An inscription over the scene (from 1475 B.C.E.) says, "Batting the ball for Hathor, who is foremost in Thebes." According to Piccione, *seker-hemat* started out as a game and evolved into a religious ritual. It was played in open courtyards of temples. Archaeologists have found three-inch, stitched leather balls that look much like the balls in the temple painting.

Like modern baseball, *seker-hemat* was a rite of spring and renewal. The player-king was seen as a strong, heroic figure, like a modern baseball star. "Sport and religion were not mutually exclusive of each other 5,000 years ago, and in many ways, they still are not today," says Piccione. Modern baseball fans would agree, especially at World Series time.

to the music. In later years, they played lyres, lutes, oboes, and tambourines—all introduced by the Hyksos.

The sistrum, a hand-held instrument of wires threaded with metal disks and beads, was used in religious rituals, to accompany everyday music, and for magical purposes. The sistrum's shaking sounds were handy for driving away demons and bringing good luck to women in childbirth. The sistrum was sacred to the goddess Hathor.

The cat goddess Bastet is often depicted rattling her sistrum, and many sistra include small cat figures.

CHAPTER 6

Egyptian Religion, Science, and Culture

TO THE EGYPTIANS, RELIGION AND MAGIC WERE "TWIN sisters." For the average person, religion meant everyday offerings and devotions honoring local deities and familiar household gods, and a deep-seated belief in the power of magical rituals, spells, charms, and protective amulets. Over the course of Egyptian history, Egyptians worshiped more than 2,000 gods and goddesses, mostly minor local deities known only in one region or village. When a city became important, so did its gods and goddesses. Egyptians were more likely to adopt foreign deities than to persecute their worshipers. They were remarkably tolerant, especially compared to other ancient peoples.

There were no universal truths, no fixed religious doctrines. The contradictions in their many views of the universe and multiple creation stories did not bother them a bit. Religion was magical, not logical. In *Ancient Egypt: Its Culture and History*, J.E. Manchip calls Egyptian religion "a huge, intricate mosaic with thousands of pieces."

The king and other high priests took care of the great matters: keeping the world running smoothly and maintaining *ma'at* in the universe. Their daily rituals ensured that the sun would rise, the inundation would occur on schedule, and crops would grow. The average family's religion was focused on humbler matters: ensuring the health and safety of children and animals, protecting the home, ensuring fertility, gaining protection from everyday dangers and troublesome spirits, and getting safely through pregnancy and childbirth. One religious story loved by king and peasant alike was the legend of Isis, Osiris, and Horus, retold in the box on page 94.

Every home had shrines to Bes, Taweret, or Bastet, fierce protectors of homes, babies, and women in childbirth. Families placed statues of

Watering the Desert
An Egyptian farmer chops cane along an irrigation ditch that channels water from the Nile River. Ancient Egyptian engineers maintained a massive, interconnected irrigation system throughout the empire.

The Osiris Legend

Osiris was the ancient king who brought civilization to Egypt. He married his sister, Isis. But his brother, Seth, also fell in love with Isis, and wanted to be king himself.

Seth tricked Osiris, then locked him in a coffin and threw it into the river. Isis, grief-stricken, searched everywhere for Osiris's body. She finally found it at Byblos (on the Mediterranean Coast in what is today Lebanon). Osiris was mummifed, and, as a mummy, impregnated Isis. She gave birth to their son, Horus.

Seth found Osiris's mummy, chopped it into pieces, and scattered the pieces throughout the Nile Valley. Once again, Isis searched. She gathered up all the pieces and reassembled them.

When Horus grew up, he set out to avenge his father's murder. In a huge battle, he injured Seth so badly that Seth became unable to father children. Seth tore out one of Horus's eyes. The earth god, Geb, declared Horus the winner of the battle and awarded him dominion over Upper and Lower Egypt. The eye of Horus that Seth tore out became the sacred *wedjat*, a powerful magical symbol of wholeness used in good luck charms.

The Osiris story was known and loved by Egyptians throughout the dynastic era. It explained why the king was entitled by the gods to rule Egypt. When a king took the throne, he became Horus and inherited the two lands that Geb had awarded Horus.

The Osiris story also offered the promise of eternal life to all people. Just as Isis had brought Osiris back to life, the gods would also bring them back to life—if they lived good lives of *ma'at*. It also inspired the practice of mummification, which was intended to make all people like Osiris.

In ancient times, coronations and jubilee festivals were often held during the Festival of Khoiakh, an annual observance of the death and resurrection of Osiris. Modern Egyptians continue this tradition by exchanging gifts of colored eggs at Sham el-Nessim, a springtime festival celebrating the rebirth of vegetation and life.

these beloved deities in wall niches, and wore amulets and charms with their images. A small statue of Bes between two cats, currently in the British Museum, probably once occupied an honored niche in the home of a workman's family. Household shrines also honored dead ancestors. If not remembered, these ghosts might stir up family trouble.

The Egyptians believed that their gods and goddesses could take any form–human, animal, a natural force (like the river), or any combination. None of the gods or goddesses was completely good, or completely evil. There was no all-evil "devil."

The Judgement of Ma'at

Even when eternal life was opened to all, it was not guaranteed. At death, each person was judged on the scales of the goddess Ma'at.

The Egyptians believed that the soul lived in the heart. When a body was mummified, most internal organs were removed and placed in canopic jars. But the heart was returned to the body with a magic charm called the *heart scarab*.

Each dead person appeared in the Hall of Ma'at for judgement. Before an audience of gods and goddesses, the heart was placed on a balance. On the other side was the Feather of Ma'at. If the person had lived a good life of *ma'at*, his heart was light as the feather, and his spirit gained eternal life. If not, a fearsome monster (part crocodile, part hippo, part lion) immediately devoured him, and he was dead forever.

Once judged fit for eternal life, the spirit faced a dangerous journey through the underworld. To get past the gatekeepers and monsters, he had to recite magic spells from the Pyramid Texts, Coffin Texts, or the Book of Going Forth by Day (also known as the Book of the Dead). Copies of these spells—illustrated scrolls for the wealthy, a few scraps of papyrus for the poor—were placed in tombs.

After death, the spirit took three different forms: *ka, ba,* and *akh*. The *ka* was the spirit of life. At the instant of death, *ka* and body were united. The *ka* stayed with the corpse. At the funeral, a ceremony called Opening of the Mouth magically activated the *ka*. The *ka* lived in the tomb, feeding on offerings of food and drink brought by the *ka* servant. In a pinch, the *ka* could magically activate food listed on menus in the tomb.

The *ba* was the spirit of personality, depicted as a human-headed bird. The *ba* could leave the body after death and roam the earth, visiting the dead person's favorite places.

The *akh* (which means "shining ghost") was the spirit of immortality. Its brightness reflected the person's accomplishments in life. Depending on the dead person's beliefs, the *akh* shone in the sky as a star, traveled with the sun in the solar boat, or lived with Osiris in the Field of Reeds—a kind of paradise afterlife.

From Predynastic times, the Egyptians believed that eternal life required preservation of the body. As tombs became larger and fancier, they contained more and richer grave goods: clothing, furniture, jewelry, pottery, toys, weapons, food and drink, and more. This caused two problems the Egyptians never completely managed to solve: preservation of corpses, and tomb robbery.

In a mastaba or pyramid, the corpse, isolated from the hot, dry desert environment that allowed natural mummification, was likely to rot. So the Egyptians invented artificial mummification. Mummies were encased in nested coffins and enclosed in stone sarcophagi. But many bodies rotted anyway. Many more were torn apart by tomb robbers, eager to get at the jewelry they were buried with.

The thought of all that buried gold, jewelry, fine linen, and luxury goods was more than some Egyptians could resist. Almost all tombs were

Egyptian Gods and Goddesses

The Egyptians recognized thousands of gods and goddesses, but here are some of the major ones:

Amun (Amun-Re): God of Thebes, associated with the goose and ram, later associated with Re and Atum. Amun-Re, Mut, and their son Khonsu were worshiped as a trio.

Anubis: Jackal-headed god, patron of embalmers, protector of tombs.

Aten: The disk of the sun, worshiped as the one true god by Akhenaten (see page 42).

Atum: Sun-god of Heliopolis, later associated with Re.

Bastet: Cat-headed goddess, protector of women, home, and children, guardian of the Delta, goddess of fertility, warmth, pleasure, the moon, and beer.

Bes: Fierce, lion-headed dwarf god, protector of children and women in childbirth.

Edjo (Wadjet): Cobra goddess, patroness of Lower Egypt, protector of the king.

Geb: Earth god.

Hapi: God of the inundation.

Hathor: Wise, gentle cow-headed goddess, protector of heaven, earth, and the underworld, beloved by wives and mothers, wet-nurse and wife of Horus, goddess of music and dance. The sistrum was her symbol. She is often shown wearing a horned sun-disk headpiece.

Heket: Frog goddess, patroness of fertility, protector of women in childbirth.

Horus: Falcon-headed sky god, son of Isis and Osiris, protector of the king.

Isis: Fertility goddess, mother of Horus, divine mourner, one of the four protectors of canopic jars, the special containers in which the internal organs removed from a mummified person were placed. The four canopic jars contained the dead person's lungs, liver, stomach, and intestines. These jars were placed in the person's tomb, often within an elaborately decorated, sealed chest.

Khepri: Creator god, shown as a scarab beetle within the sun disk.

Khnum: Ram-headed god; he created the earth and the first man on his potter's wheel.

Khonsu: Warrior god, son of Amun-Re and Mut.

looted, many within days of burial. The Egyptians tried to foil tomb robbers with burial chambers made of solid quartzite topped with multi-ton rock slabs. They tried false doors, trap doors, mazes, dead-end passages, dummy chambers, trick doors, hidden shafts, stairways leading nowhere, passages back-filled with huge stone blocks and rubble, curses inscribed on walls, Medjay guards. Nothing worked.

After the pyramids were looted, Egypt's kings decided their mummies might be safer in caves carved into solid rock. But the rock-cut

Ma'at: Goddess of balance, order, and justice who judged souls after death. Her symbol was an ostrich feather.

Min: Fat, jovial, popular fertility god.

Montu: Falcon-headed war god of the king.

Mut: Wife of Amun-Re.

Neith: Hunting goddess of Sais, one of the four protectors of canopic jars. Her symbol was two feathered arrows.

Nehkbet: Vulture goddess of Upper Egypt, protector of the king.

Nephthys: Sister of Isis, Osiris, and Seth, divine mourner, one of four protectors of canopic jars.

Nun: God of chaos who existed before creation of the world.

Nut: Sky goddess, wife of earth god Geb; her arched body forms the sky.

Osiris: God of the underworld, the dead, the land's fertility, and the inundation. Depicted as a mummified king, he offered eternal life to all.

Ptah: Creator god of Memphis, patron of artisans and craftsmen.

Re: Sun god of Heliopolis, later merged with Atum and Amun.

Sekhmet: Fierce lion-headed goddess, she destroyed Egypt's enemies.

Sebek: Crocodile god, associated with Seth.

Selkit: Scorpion goddess, one of the four protectors of canopic jars.

Seshat: Goddess of writing, the divine librarian, wife of Thoth.

Seth: God of disorder, storms, violence, and mischief, brother and murderer of Osiris.

Shu: Air god, paired with Tefnut, he was usually shown between Geb (earth) and Nut (sky).

Sopdu: Bearded guardian god of Egypt's eastern borders.

Taweret: Pregnant hippopotamus, protector of fertility and women in childbirth.

Tefnut: Moisture goddess, paired with Shu.

Thoth: Ibis-headed god, husband of Seshat, vizier and scribe of the gods, inventor of writing, mathematics, languages, accounting, magic, law, and board games. He controlled the moon, stars, and seasons.

Upuaut: Jackal god, avenger of Osiris, protector of the dead, opener of the ways into the underworld.

A Mummy Priestess
This coffin and mummy were for a priestess, and date from about 1000 B.C.E. They are now in the British Museum in London. Our word mummy *comes from the Arab word* mumiyah, *which means "tar" or "pitch."*

tombs in the Valley of the Kings, in the cliffs west of Thebes, presented no real difficulties for tomb robbers.

The graves of ordinary folks were seldom targets for looters—there was nothing much to steal. Poor people were buried like their ancestors, in simple reed-lined pits in the sand. In many cases, their bodies probably lasted longer than most expensively mummified kings.

At Home in the Afterlife

Much of what is known about Egyptian life comes from tombs: paintings, murals and carvings of everyday activities, statues of the tomb owner and his family and animals, food and drink, including "magical menus," and household equipment and supplies. Detailed wooden models of typical home and farm scenes placed in the tomb—kitchens, breweries, workshops, gardens, and boats—could be magically activated as needed. The houses of the living were recreated in the houses of the dead.

During the Old Kingdom, the companions the king chose to accompany him in eternal life were not permitted to sail the skies with him in the solar boat. They were confined to their tombs, which is why they went to so much trouble and expense to store away plenty of food, drink, and luxury goods.

Once the afterlife was opened to all after the Old Kingdom, the king still ascended to the heavens after death. Everyone else was no longer confined to spending eternity in their tombs, and enjoyed the afterlife of their choosing. For the elite, this was comfort and luxury, with the goods they had brought along in their well-equipped tombs—just like the villas and palaces they enjoyed on earth, only better. Farmers and peasants also pictured the ideal afterlife much like earthly life, without the bad parts. In the afterlife's Field of Reeds it was never too hot, there was no illness or injury, flies did not bite, the inundation was always just right, and grain grew 15 feet high.

The spirits of the dead required daily nourishment. Bakers, brewers, and other *ka* servants who lived in necropolis villages prepared and served

How Mummies Were Made

Herodotus, in his *Histories*, described mummification. The dead person's family approached an embalmer, who offered three levels of service. He displayed small models so the family could see how the mummy would look, and they agreed on a price.

For the top-of-the-line mummification, the skull was first cleaned by removing the brain through the nose using a long, thin iron hook. The skull cavity was then rinsed with chemicals.

Then, using a flint knife, the embalmer made a large incision in the abdomen. The lungs, liver, stomach, and intestines were removed and washed in a chemical bath. These organs were then packed, along with spices and natron (a sodium mineral used for drying), into four canopic jars, for placement in the dead person's tomb under the care of goddesses Isis, Nephthys, Neith, and Selkit.

Finally, the heart was removed and the emptied torso was cleaned with palm wine and fragrant spices. When it was ready, the heart was placed back into the chest cavity, along with a heart scarab. (Often made of gold and jewels, this was a favorite target of tomb robbers, who hacked open mummies to get them.)

The mostly empty torso was now filled with rolls of linen, sawdust, and a mixture of myrrh, cassia, spices, and natron. The body was repacked and padded until the embalmer achieved what he felt was a natural look.

For special corpses, such as kings, there were extra steps to be taken at this point. For example, When Rameses II was mummified, his nose was packed with peppercorns to preserve its unique shape, his fingernails and hair were colored with henna—a natural reddish dye, symbol of life—and his abdominal incision was covered with a solid gold plaque.

For all mummies, the next step was to stitch up the incision in the torso. Now the body had to be dried. The embalmer laid out the body on a six-foot-wide table covered with natron, and piled more natron over the body to cover it completely.

After 70 days of drying, the body was uncovered, thoroughly washed, and anoint it with precious oils and fragrant ointments. Then is was wrapped head to toe in several layers of fine linen strips soaked in gum. The fingers and toes were wrapped individually, and for really expensive mummifications solid gold toenail and fingernail covers were put in place, and the tongue was replaced with a solid gold artificial tongue. During the wrapping process, amulets, charms, and scraps of papyrus with magical spells were placed between the layers of linen.

For less-expensive mummification, the embalmer simply injected oil of cedar into the corpse and packed it in natron. The oil dissolved everything but the skin and bones. After 70 days, the oil was drained off, carrying away the dissolved flesh. The dried corpse was then returned to the family for burial, with no linen wrapping.

daily meals to the spirits. These practical *ka* servants removed the food at the end of each day and took it home for supper. In case *ka* servants neglected their duties, every prudent tomb owner had menus of his favorite meals inscribed on the walls of his tomb. In a pinch, his *ka* could magically bring the menu items into existence.

A modern Egyptian tradition called el-Arbeiyin recalls these ancient beliefs. After a person has been dead for 40 days, family members bring food to his grave and distribute it to poor people who have gathered there.

Agriculture: Backbone of the Economy

Egypt's agricultural economy was built on a technique known as basin cultivation. Natural depressions flooded by the inundation were surrounded with berms and dams to hold in water. Canals let water in or out as needed. In times of prosperity, land was reclaimed from the desert and marsh and was converted to farmland.

The inundation often destroyed or moved boundary markers and damaged or destroyed canals, berms, ponds, and dams. Once the floodwaters receded, farmers helped government officials re-survey croplands. Damaged systems had to be rebuilt or repaired swiftly, so planting could begin.

The recently soaked fields needed little or no plowing. The farmer scattered seeds and turned his animals and children loose in the fields to trample it in. A farmer's tools were simple: primitive picks and hoes, baskets, and heavy pottery water jars carried on yokes across the shoulders. Farmers grew two kinds of wheat, emmer (*Triticum dicoccum*) and spelt (*Triticum spelta*). They also grew several varieties of barley (*Hordeum vulgare*), mostly for beer. Farmers worked together to harvest one field after another as quickly as possible, using wood sickles with flint blades. It was hot, backbreaking work, lightened by competitions, work songs, and many jars of beer. The grain sheaves were gathered into bundles and carried by donkeys to the threshing floor in the village.

Emmer and spelt both require vigorous threshing (beating the grains out of their husks) before they can be ground into coarse flour. Animals and children trampled the grain to separate out the husks. The grain was tossed into the air and the lighter husks blew away. The heavier grains fell into large, flat baskets and were filtered through coarse sieves to remove pebbles and insects. Husks and stems were saved for making mudbrick. The grain was measured, packed into sacks, and stored in silos, awaiting the tax collector.

MEMOS TO MUMMIES TO MUSEUMS

Many of the ancient Egyptian papyri held by Duke University in Durham, North Carolina, came from mummy cartonnage from a cemetery near Herakleopolis, south of modern Cairo. Cartonnage is a covering of several layers of papyrus paper used on some Late Period mummies. After being wrapped with linen strips, the mummy was covered with sheets of cartonnage and coated with a thick layer of plaster. The papyri used for cartonnage often came from recycling bins in Egyptian government and administrative offices.

The third major crop was flax (*Linum usitatissimum*). Bundles of flax fibers were carried off to be prepared for spinning, weaving into cloth, and braiding into rope—after the tax collector had taken his cut.

Crime and Punishment

Egyptians were courteous, law-abiding people. Society was generally orderly and peaceful. Men and women were treated equally by law and custom, as were members of different social classes.

Egyptian law was based on custom, tradition, and *ma'at*. An offense against law and order was an offense against *ma'at*. Laws covered crimes, land disputes, commercial transactions, wills, property transfers, and trusts for eternal care of tombs. Legal disputes could be complex. One land dispute among several generations of a feuding wealthy family went on for decades, with many trials presided over by a series of viziers.

All judgements were made in the king's name. There were no professional lawyers. Trials were speedy and punishments were swift. Imprisonment was considered expensive and unproductive. Prisons were used as courts, storehouses for legal records, and to hold prisoners awaiting trial. The death penalty was rare. It had to be approved by the king and was reserved for only the most horrible crimes. Children who killed their parents faced especially gruesome deaths, such as being eaten alive by crocodiles. A merciful king might allow a condemned criminal to commit suicide.

For serious offenses, a criminal would have his nose or ears, or both, cut off. He might also be sentenced to hard labor in the mines of Nubia, or be banished to a faraway frontier fort. Disgrace and banishment were considered worse than death. For lesser crimes, beatings and whippings were common. Occasionally, an entire family was punished for a relative's crime.

While this all may sound harsh to us today, Egypt's laws and punishments were generally much more humane and enlightened than those of most other ancient cultures.

Weapons of War

The Egyptians were not warriors by nature. Their battle gear was mostly adapted from hunting weapons. Soldiers used bows, spears, javelins, and daggers, and carried animal-hide shields. Much of the Egyptian army was made up of foreign mercenaries who favored their own traditional weapons and protective gear.

The Tax Collector's Haul

The Egyptians were among the first civilizations to pay taxes. Taxes were heavy, about 50 percent of all produce, plus a head tax on each person. Taxes were paid "in kind," which means in raw materials and finished goods. Some professionals paid taxes in labor.

Egyptians did not use money until very late in their history. Instead of writing a check or authorizing an electronic payment, they hauled their taxes in sacks. A tax collector's storehouse might contain:

barley in sacks	worked wood	balls of frankincense	jars of wine and beer
dates	flax in bundles	salt	bolts of linen cloth
flour	papyrus scrolls	wigs	dyes and paints
cakes	bundles of papyrus	charcoal	leather sandals
dried fish	dressed animal hides	kohl (eye make-up)	chariots

During the New Kingdom, the Egyptians became famous for their khepesh swords—curved scimitars shaped like the leg of a bull. The king often carried this weapon. The Hyksos introduced the horse and chariot, which the Egyptians used mainly for speed. Their chariots were lightweight wicker vehicles that carried a driver and an archer or spear thrower. In battle, chariots were deployed in large groups. Diplomats and couriers also used chariots for speedy travel.

Mathematics

The Egyptians were interested in practical applications of mathematics, not theories. They were very good at manipulating numbers, and used their skill to solve real world problems faced on the job by engineers, tax collectors, construction supervisors, and military officers. The major surviving Egyptian mathematical document, the Rhind Papyrus, is a collection of mathematical problems with solutions.

The Egyptians multiplied by repeated addition, and divided by repeated subtraction. They used fractions, but only with a one in the numerator. They did not know about the concept of zero.

They used a hieroglyphic decimal system. Units were represented by vertical strokes arranged in rows. A spiral represented 100, 200 was two spirals, 10,000 was a finger, 100,000 was a tadpole. A god with upraised arms meant 1 million—or "I can count no further."

Accounting, bookkeeping, surveying, and land measurement were highly sophisticated. Accountant-scribes knew how to determine accurate property boundaries and calculate crop yields based on land area. They could estimate labor and materials for construction projects, and determine consumption rates for food and other commodities for districts, based on population.

They were skilled at drawing plans and making accurate layouts. For designing complexes of buildings, they used a primitive theodolite, a surveying instrument that measures angles. They used practical mathematics to figure out the best ways to transport and erect huge blocks of stone, massive obelisks, and colossal statues.

Astronomy

The Egyptians were practical astronomers, too, using the stars mainly to orient buildings and for timekeeping. When Khufu built the Great Pyramid, Egyptian astronomy was at its height. An Egyptian catalog of the universe lists five constellations, including crocodile, ox leg (the modern Great Bear), and Osiris holding a staff (the modern Orion).

Egyptian astronomers divided the heavenly bodies into "unwearied stars" (planets), "imperishable stars" (stars always visible above the horizon), and "indestructible stars" (fixed stars). They knew Jupiter, Saturn, Mars, Venus, and possibly Mercury.

They divided each day into 24 hours. The duration of each hour varied with the season. They used sundials, shadow clocks, and water clocks, marking time by measuring shadows or dripping water.

Health and Medicine

Egypt's physicians were famous for their knowledge and skill. The Greeks, Romans, Persians, and Arabs admired and borrowed Egyptian medical practices.

Doctors treated problems common at farms and construction sites: stiffness, sprains, crushing injuries, fractures, wounds, burns, and skin disorders. They used splints, bandages, and compresses, and performed amputations and simple surgeries with saws, knives, drills, hooks, and forceps. The Edwin Smith Papyrus (from about 1600 B.C.E.), a kind of casebook for surgeons, divides injuries and disorders of the head and chest into treatable, non-treatable, and "maybe" cases.

Although medicine and embalming (preparing the dead for burial) were closely related, Egyptians had little understanding of the internal

CONNECTIONS >>>>>>>>>>>>

Artesian Wells

Egyptian engineers maintained the empire's massive, interconnected irrigation system, and expanded it, using fired mud-brick or copper drainpipes and drain tiles to convert low-lying areas into productive farmland. They were skilled well-drillers. A well near the Great Pyramid, dug about 3000 B.C.E., bores through 300 feet of solid rock before reaching water.

In a land where water management was a matter of life and death, Egyptian engineers were noted for their ability to locate sources of fresh water deep beneath the desert sands and bring it to the surface. They were the first to use percussion drilling (pounding a sharpened bit into rock with a series of powerful blows) to drill artesian wells, in which water is forced up by its own pressure from pockets deep underground.

Artesian wells are still common, especially in rural areas. Percussion drilling is still widely used for drilling water wells and in gas, oil, and mineral exploration. Modern drill rigs use compressed air, lasers, and other high-tech equipment, but it all started with determined Egyptian engineers pounding rocks.

workings of the human body. Corpses were sacred—not to be studied or dissected.

Although Herodotus considered the residents of Upper Egypt the healthiest people in the world, mummies and skeletons show that Egyptians suffered many ills. Most had rotten teeth. Their bread, full of sand and grit from grinding stones, wore down their tooth enamel until the roots were exposed, causing abscesses and severe pain.

Except for uncomplicated treatments such as setting fractures and stitching wounds, magic spells and amulets were the best remedies Egyptian doctors had for most ailments. Diseases were blamed on demons or ghosts. Prescriptions called for applying potions while reciting magical spells and incantations. Potions included mixtures of leaves, herbs, fruit juices, dates and figs, honey, tannic acid, resins, castor oil, human milk, animal fat and blood, animal fur, snake grease, and goose grease.

Language and Writing

Hieroglyphics, Egyptian picture-writing, was used for almost 35 centuries for religious texts and inscriptions on monuments. (Today, you can visit web sites to find out what your name looks like in hieroglyphics; see page 122.) The earliest hieroglyphics, ownership and business records, appear on stone vases and seals.

But hieroglyphics quickly became too cumbersome for everyday use. A flowing, script-like writing called hieratic (from the Greek word *hieratikos*, which means "priestly"), derived from hieroglyphics, was used for almost all writing. Later, busy scribes invented shorthand, called demotic (from the Greek word *demotikos*, "popular"). At the end of the dynastic era, a script derived from the Greek alphabet, called Coptic, came into wide use.

Egypt's best-known literary works are collections of magical spells to aid the dead in their passage through the dangerous underworld on their way to eternal life. In the Old Kingdom, spells called the Pyramid Texts were inscribed on the walls of royal tombs. In the Middle Kingdom, similar spells, the Coffin Texts, were painted or carved on coffins.

The most famous collection of religious-magical literature is called the Book of Going Forth by Day, sometimes known as the Book of the Dead. It includes 90 chapters of magical spells that were copied on papyrus scrolls and placed in tombs. Many surviving copies are beautifully illustrated in color. A rich man might have an illustrated scroll 120 feet long, with spells covering every danger. A poor man would get just a spell or two on a scrap of papyrus.

The Middle Kingdom was the golden age of non-religious literature. Teachers loved the "wisdom literature," collections of proverbs and instructions for living a life of *ma'at*. Stories such as *The Tale of Sinuhe, The Tale of the Eloquent Peasant,* and *The Shipwrecked Sailor* were so popular that they were copied and repeated for centuries. The moral of many of these stories was, "There's no place like home." In the New Kingdom, love poetry also became popular.

CONNECTIONS >>>>>>>>>>>

A Calendar That Lasted

The Egyptians invented the 365-day calendar. They actually used three calendars: a lunar agricultural calendar tied to the seasons, a civil calendar based on the 365-day year, and a lunar religious calendar based on the moon but tied to the civil calendar.

The agricultural year had three seasons of four months each. The seasons were *akhet* (inundation), *peret* (germination, growth), and *shemu* (warm season, harvest, and possibly the source of our word "summer"). New year's day, the first day of akhet, occurred each summer when the star Sopdet (Sirius) rose precisely at sunrise.

The civil year had 360 days, divided into 12 months of 30 days each. Each month had three 10-day weeks called *decades*. To make 365, five days were added, celebrated as the birthdays of five gods.

Misalignments between the calendars made keeping track of religious festivals (often tied to phases of the moon) difficult, so the Egyptians also invented a lunar religious calendar.

The inconsistencies among their calendars did not trouble the Egyptians. Their great insight into calendar making was that any calendar is artificial, so it might as well be simple, practical, and useful. Multiple calendars worked fine for them for 3,000 years.

The calendar we use today traces its roots to the Egyptian civil calendar. When Julius Caesar needed a simple, accurate calendar for the Roman Empire, that is the one he chose.

The Rosetta Stone
This famous stone, dating from 196 B.C.E. and discovered in 1799, was the key to understanding Egyptian hieroglyphics. The same text appears in hieroglyphics on top, then demotic, then Greek.

Collections of papyri (stored in boxes and pottery jars) in private homes and temple schools were called Houses of Life. These libraries served religious and practical purposes, containing papyri of religious, scientific, and popular literature.

Arts and Artisans

Art was created for religious, symbolic, or magical purposes, not artistic expression. Each part of a scene had to convey the exact message intended. Though most scenes were stereotyped set pieces based on conventional themes, the best Egyptian art works are still graceful and lively.

Egyptian artists were careful observers of nature and excellent draftsmen. But in depicting people, they followed long-established traditions, conventions, and proportions. Heads appear in profile, eyes are face-on. Torsos turn toward the viewer, legs are twisted into profile. All five fingers are extended and visible. Nobles are larger than commoners. Men are larger than women. Children are tiny, but with adult proportions. The king is always much bigger than anyone else. Everything is drawn literally and exactly, with bold outlines and no shading or shadows. There is no doubt about the scene's subject and purpose.

Each scene was carefully planned and designed. The artist sketched a grid on his surface and laid out figures with traditional proportions (see page 22). As long as he followed the conventions, he was free to arrange people and objects as he liked.

The Egyptians loved vibrant color. Paints, manufactured from minerals and plants, included black (from lead ore and lampblack), blue and green (from malachite and copper), white (from limestone), and brown, red, and yellow (from colored earth and plants). Colors had religious and symbolic meanings. People were painted either red-brown (men) or yellow (women) to indicate they were alive, or green or black if they were dead. Osiris was green, Amun-Re blue. Other gods had yellow skin because their flesh was made of gold. White symbolized hope or pleasure. Red meant evil.

Most statues were idealized forms, not personal portraits. They were designed for specific settings, such as a tomb or temple. Sculptors worked with mostly stone-age tools, in alabaster, basalt, diorite, granite, limestone, marble, and quartzite. Eyes were made of white quartz, rock crystal, ebony, and copper for a lifelike quality. Many sculptures were painted. The painted limestone bust of Nefertiti in the Berlin Museum is among the world's most famous sculptures.

In early Predynastic times, the Nile valley still had some large trees, and woodworking achieved its highest level. Later woodworkers were at a disadvantage because of the lack of good quality large timber. Native woods were available only in small sizes and quantities. Imported wood—cedar, cypress, ebony, juniper, fir, yew, and oak—was used for columns, temple doors, flagpoles, fine coffins, furniture, and seagoing ships.

The Key to Hieroglyphics

In 1799, a stone tablet was discovered at Rosetta, in the Nile Delta. On this stone, (which came to be known as the Rosetta Stone), the same message appears in three languages: hieroglyphics, demotic, and Greek. Greek was well known, so the key to hieroglyphics seemed at hand. Scholars worked furiously, but made little progress. In 1822, French scholar Jean-Francois Champollion (1790–1832) hit on the key concept that hieroglyphic writing is neither purely ideographic (each sign standing for an idea) nor purely phonetic (each sign representing a sound). It is a combination of both.

A word was spelled out in phonetic symbols. At the end, a final picture was added. This last symbol was not supposed to be read with the other signs, but was an ideogram—a pictorial clue to the word's meaning. Vowels were not written. So the word *deshret* (desert), for example, was written with the pictograms for *d-sh-r-t*.

Hieroglyphics are beautifully designed drawings of birds, animals, people, buildings, and everyday objects. Throughout most of Egyptian history, 600 to 700 individual hieroglyphic symbols were in use. The last known hieroglyphic inscription was carved on a temple wall at Philae in the year 394. Knowledge of hieroglyphics was then lost—until 1822. Today, the phrase "Rosetta Stone" is used to refer to anything that is key to unlocking a mystery of communication.

Clay-heavy Nile mud was the raw material for most pottery. Beer and wine jars, oil vessels, mugs, plates, cosmetic pots, canopic jars, figurines, *ushabtis*, and most coffins were made of mud "coarseware." The types and styles of coarseware found at ancient sites provide important clues for establishing dates and chronologies.

Faience (quartz or clay covered with a fired glaze) was popular in Egypt as far back as the Early Dynastic Period. The Step Pyramid of Djoser has inlaid faience tiles. It was used for amulets, small objects such as bowls and statuettes, and inlays. The most popular colors were blue and greenish blue, recalling the Egyptians' favorite gemstones, lapis lazuli and turquoise.

Beginning in the Eighteenth Dynasty, artisans cut and molded glass to create beads, amulets, perfume jars, vases, and figurines in a rainbow of colors. Glassblowing, forming molten glass into intricate shapes, was unknown in dynastic times.

Jewelry for the wealthy was made of gold, hammered, cut, or shaped, and adorned with gemstones: amethysts, turquoise, rock crystal, malachite, lapis lazuli, onyx, peridot, hematite, jade, coral, carnelian, garnet, jasper, agate, beryl, and rare emeralds from the eastern desert. Amulets and ornaments of faience, bone, and pottery were mass-produced for ordinary folks. Silver was rare and little used. Electrum, a rare, highly-prized natural alloy of gold and silver, came mostly from Upper Egypt and Nubia. Much of the work of Egyptian jewelers was sealed up in tombs, stolen, and melted down by looters. The surviving pieces only hint at the fabulous treasures that were lost.

Textiles

Most flax was spun and woven into linen cloth for clothing and domestic textiles. Torn into strips, fine linen wrapped mummified corpses. Flax was also spun and braided into durable rope, strong enough to haul multi-ton stone blocks.

Linen was one of Egypt's major exports, in demand all over the world. It was woven in several grades, from coarse cloth to fine, almost transparent "royal linen" prized by wealthy ladies. Most linen was left its natural, off-white shade. Vegetable dyes were used to make yellow (safflower), red (madder), and blue (acacia tree bark) fabric.

In Predynastic times, the art of weaving fine linen on flat, horizontal looms was already well-developed. The Hyksos introduced vertical looms. During the Nineteenth Dynasty, a major linen manufacturing

---

TOOLS WITHOUT IRON

For most of the dynastic era, Egyptians used tools and weapons made of flint, wood, copper and some bronze. Copper, from Nubia and the Sinai, was their primary industrial metal. By the New Kingdom, the Egyptians had learned to make bronze by adding tin to copper. They did not use iron as an industrial metal until the Twenty-first Dynasty, long after it had come into common use in the Near East.

business was run by harem ladies and minor members of the royal family at a royal palace at Miwer in the Delta.

Silk, a luxury reserved for only the wealthiest ladies, was not known until the Persian conquest in 525 B.C.E. Cotton, for which modern Egypt is famous, was not grown until Roman times.

CONNECTIONS >>>>>>>>>>>>>>>>>>>>>>>>>>>>>

Papermaking

Papyrus paper was made in single sheets and in long scrolls. Our word "paper" comes from the Egyptian word *pa-pe-yo,* "that [plant] of the Nile."

The papyrus plant (*Cyperous papyrus*) grew in great quantities in the Nile shallows and in the swamps and wetlands surrounding the river, especially in the Delta. Papyrus was a forerunner of paper, although unlike true paper (which was invented by the Chinese), it is a laminated material (made in layers).

Trusting to their amulets and magical spells, harvesters waded into crocodile-infested wetlands to gather it for the paper upon which their bureaucratic government depended. When demand increased, they grew papyrus as a crop.

Egyptian papyrus makers cut the triangular papyrus stalks into thin strips, which they softened by soaking in muddy water. They then layered the flattened strips horizontally and vertically into a kind of mat, and pounded them together into a thin laminate. Finally, they smoothed and polished the papyrus with a stone or bone. The result was a smooth, portable, lightweight, inexpensive, and reasonably durable writing surface that took ink rapidly and well. Egyptians were already making papyrus by 4000 B.C.E., and the oldest written papyrus rolls are 5,000 years old. Because the papyrus plant was common in Egypt and rare elsewhere, papyrus was, for a long time, an Egyptian monopoly. It was coveted all over the known world. Throughout the dynastic era and after, papyrus was one of Egypt's chief exports. The availability of Egyptian papyrus helped encourage the development and advance of writing in many cultures around the Mediterranean.

Papyrus fell out of use by the ninth century C.E., replaced by more elegant (and much more expensive) parchment. The cost and scarcity of parchment put the written word out of the reach of most people—even educated people.

Just as papyrus was readily available to every Egyptian who could read and write, today inexpensive paper is easily available to all. The average American uses about 700 pounds of paper products each year. Ironically, papyrus is no longer grown in Egypt.

Epilogue

TODAY, THE ARAB REPUBLIC OF EGYPT IS HOME TO MORE THAN 72 million people. Most are jam-packed into the same 550-mile-long narrow canyon that supported no more that 3 to 4 million people at the height of Egypt's ancient empire. More than 45 percent of Egyptians live in a few huge cities, such as Cairo (10 million) and Alexandria (4 million). Agriculture employs 29 percent of Egyptians. Another 22 percent work in industry; 49 percent staff service industries.

Modern Egypt's boundaries have not changed much since ancient times. Egypt is bordered by Libya on the west, Sudan in the south, and Israel on the northeast. Most of Egypt's land area is barren, desolate desert. Only 2 percent (less than 8,000 square miles) of Egypt's 385,000-square-mile area can be farmed. Almost all of it is intensively cultivated.

Modern Egypt shows little trace of ancient Egyptian culture. It is culturally and religiously an Arab, Islamic nation. More than 90 percent of Egyptians profess the Moslem (mostly Sunni) faith. A small community (perhaps 10 percent of the population) of Coptic Christians thrives, and areas of southern and middle Egypt are heavily Coptic.

Egypt is a democracy and a secular country, and most Egyptians practice a moderate, progressive form of Islam. However, Egypt is facing pressure from more traditional, conservative groups who would like to see Islam have more influence over day-to-day affairs. Conservative Muslims worry that Western influences will weaken and eventually erase the traditions that have persisted in Islamic countries for centuries. Moderate Muslims worry that Egypt will become a theocracy (a nation ruled by religious officials). The conflict is ongoing and has, at times, turned violent.

OPPOSITE
An Islamic Nation
Egyptians gather for Friday prayers on the first day of the Muslim holy month of Ramadan at the Al-Azhar mosque in Cairo. More than 90 percent of Egyptians today are Muslim.

Fashionable Tourists
Early in the 1900s, traveling to Egypt to see the antiquities was considered fashionable, especially for wealthy Europeans. These tourists often climbed all over the ancient ruins and even brought back souvenirs they chiseled off. Today, visits to ancient sites are carefully supervised.

Both Christians and Muslims speak Arabic, in a variety of regional dialects. Many educated Egyptians are fluent in French and English. Only 51 percent of the population can read and write–a big jump over ancient figures (2 to 5 percent) but still well below most of the developed world.

Like literacy, life expectancy has increased since ancient times. Men can expect to live to 60, women to 66.2 (ancients did well hoping for age 30). But it still lags far behind the developed world. Infant mortality is almost 60 per 1,000 live births–61st highest in the world. With fewer than 2 million motor vehicles in the country, it is clear that many Egyptians still get around the way their ancestors did–on foot and donkeys.

Egypt's major industries are textiles, food production, and tourism. A $3.9 billion dollar per year industry, tourism is dependent mainly upon ancient ruins and monuments, many of which are now threatened by rising water tables and salt retention–not to mention looting. Egypt's location at the crossroads of the troubled Middle East, and some well-publicized violent incidents, have also threatened the vital flow of tourists. So far, worldwide fascination with ancient Egyptian culture has overcome tourists' nervousness.

The Plunder Continues

Tomb robbing is an ancient tradition. Merykare, king during the troubled First Intermediate Period, admitted to his son that even he had looted tombs.

Ancient and medieval tomb robbers melted down uncounted gold objects. They ripped apart mummies to find jeweled amulets. They destroyed or vandalized inscriptions and paintings. Later religious sects considered the ancients misguided pagans, so they destroyed temples and monuments. Temples were converted to Christian churches or Muslim mosques.

The builders of medieval Cairo stripped the fine white limestone casings off the pyramids. Early Arab explorers, unable to find an entrance into the Great Pyramid, broke in by heating the surface with huge fires, then pouring on cold vinegar. Battering rams made short work of the shattered rocks.

French-Italian Bernadino Drovetti (1776-1852), one of the most ambitious looters, amassed huge collections of antiquities, which he sold to museums in Sardinia, Turin, Paris (The Louvre), and Prussia. Agents for Western cities transported massive obelisks, sarcophagi, and monumental sculptures across the ocean to new homes in parks and urban squares.

Plunder of building stone and treasure continued well into the 1800s. In *The Search for Ancient Egypt*, archaeologist Jean Vercoutter reports that "between 1820 and 1828, 13 entire temples disappeared, their stones either used to build factories or ending up in lime kilns; and no one will ever know how many statues and reliefs suffered the same fate."

Many looted artifacts eventually arrived in the hands of scholars who could properly care for them. Vercoutter comments, "The objects that were pillaged... were at least preserved for posterity." But much was tragically destroyed in the rush for treasure. In an effort to stop the plundering, the Egyptian government established its Antiquities Service and founded the Cairo Museum in 1835.

Despite heroic efforts by Egyptian authorities, the plunder continues. It is illegal to remove antiquities from Egypt, or to sell them. Thousands of sites are under constant guard, and due to this strong enforcement of laws, antiquities smuggling is not as extensive as it is in other areas of the world. But all Egypt is one large archaeological site. Modern thieves drive right up to ancient tombs with pickup trucks and chainsaws.

Many Egyptians are very poor. Government funds for security are not plentiful. The price of Egyptian antiquities on the international black market continues to rise. The temptations are enormous. Objects have even disappeared from display cases in the Cairo Museum.

Museum storerooms throughout Egypt are jam-packed with artifacts, many never properly documented, catalogued, or even counted. Even some archaeologists cannot resist the temptation. In the summer of 2003, an archaeologist was caught at the Cairo airport leaving the country with a suitcase full of small objects.

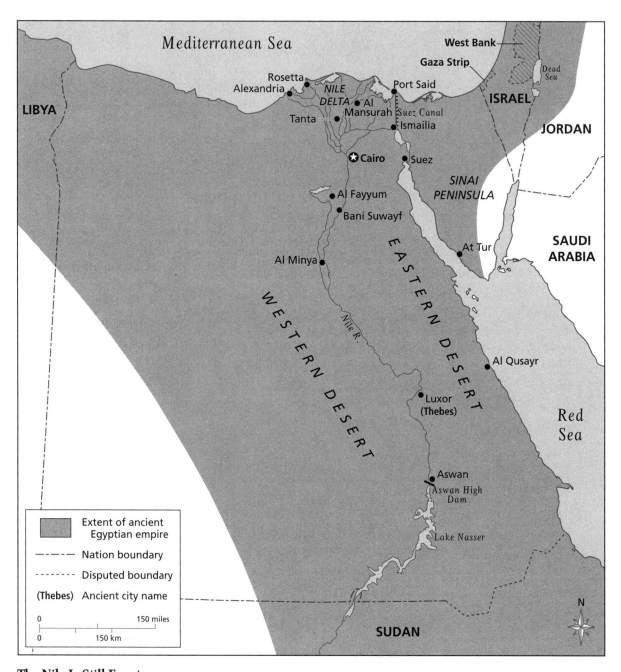

The Nile Is Still Egypt

An ancient Egyptian would recognize this modern map of Egypt, with its major cities still clustered around the life-giving waters of the Nile River.

The Aswan High Dam

The completion of the Aswan High Dam in 1965 was a turning point for Egypt. The dam brought total control over the Nile's famously unpredictable inundation, turning the river into a long irrigation canal. But just like the river in its natural state, the dam has been both a blessing and a curse for Egypt.

The dam enables Egyptians to store two to three years of Nile flow for controlled release for irrigation. This has been a great benefit to agriculture and health, protecting Egypt from massive droughts in 1972–1973 and 1983–1984. The dam also saved Egypt from catastrophic floods in 1964 and 1973. Crops can now be grown year-round. The dam immediately provided irrigation for more than 1 million acres of new farmland. Egypt now has many more options for siting towns and factories—a great benefit to industry. The dam also generates 2,500 megawatts of electricity without using fossil fuels.

On the other hand, the loss of the more than 100 million tons of sediment per year that the Nile used to carry has caused severe coastal erosion. The Nile bloom—a rich soup of nutrients that used to flow into the

Damming the Nile
The Aswan High Dam has brought a mixture of good and bad. The Nile's annual flood can now be controlled, but many antiquities have been flooded and there have been grave ecological consequences, as well.

Ancient Bones

This 2,660-year-old coffin of an Egyptian child was uncovered in 1996 at an archaeological dig near Djoser's step pyramid, 19 miles south of Cairo.

Mediterranean Sea and feed marine life—is now only a memory. Egypt's formerly productive coastal sardine, anchovy, and shrimp fisheries have collapsed. The eastern Mediterranean basin is all but lifeless. Coastal land is vanishing, and without new deposits of sediment, parts of the Nile Delta are sinking. The amount of water that reaches the sea from the Nile is now less than 5 percent of the natural flow.

One effect seen immediately upon the dam's completion was the loss of raw materials (Nile mud) for making mud-brick—a major local industry. Farmers started selling their topsoil to brick makers, gaining short-term profit at the expense of the long-term productivity of their land.

Without the yearly deposit of natural fertilizer from the inundation, Egyptian farmers turned to expensive artificial inorganic fertilizers, which they need to apply in ever-increasing quantities. More than 30 percent of the dam's electricity generating capacity runs factories that produce artificial fertilizer.

Meanwhile, sediment is building up in Lake Nasser at an alarming rate: 100 million tons per year. Projections say that within 600 years, half the lake's capacity to store irrigation water will be lost. Within 1,000 years, the lake will be useless for water storage. (In the context of Egypt's history, 1,000 years is not a long time.) There is no known, realistic way to remove the sediments already trapped behind the dam.

Because of the constant supply of irrigation water to croplands, Egypt's water table has risen dramatically, threatening many ancient tombs, monuments, archaeological digs, and popular tourist destinations. Because the river no longer washes away excess salts, the land is in danger of becoming too salty, further threatening both agriculture and ancient structures.

To counter this threat, the dam's distribution system includes a complex network of channels and drainage canals to remove excess salts and water. Huge electric pumps empty these into the Mediterranean Sea. These pumps use another 5 to 10 percent of the electricity generated by the dam.

A Looming Food Crisis

Egypt's chief export crop is cotton (not grown in ancient times). Rice, beans, fruits, wheat, vegetables, and corn are also grown. Modern Egyptian agriculture is spectacularly efficient. Food production per acre is almost the highest in the world. Since the dam was built, nearly all available water is used to irrigate crops. All potential cropland is already intensively cultivated. But Egyptian food production is still not sufficient to meet the needs of its ever-growing population. In fact, Egypt imports three-quarters of the wheat it consumes.

Egypt's population has tripled since the end of World War II, and is projected to double again by the end of the 21st century. In the early days after the dam was built, Egypt could buy enough wheat with revenues from exported cotton. But by the 1980s, Egypt had one of the highest rates of wheat import per person of any country in the world. Egypt can no longer grow enough cotton to buy the wheat it needs, so it sells oil. But Egypt has a growing domestic demand for its own, already-depleted, oil reserves.

Delicate Digging

Before a modern Egyptologist moves a spoonful of sand, he spends years planning his proposed dig and securing permission from the Supreme Council of Antiquities. Satellite and aerial photographs, ground-penetrating radar, sonar, robotic probes, and other remote sensing equipment can explore sites without disturbing them. To minimize unnecessary digging, special drills send thin, transparent tubes into the ground, bringing back cores—long, narrow samples of the soil beneath. The cores reveal how many layers of soil are present, and if any have been disturbed.

Site work proceeds with the greatest care and patience. A site is mapped, measured, and marked. Each layer is analyzed. Nothing is moved until it has been inspected, photographed, measured, documented, and catalogued. All artifacts—from gold statues to pottery fragments—are packed and stored carefully. Archaeologists are painfully aware that objects preserved underground for millennia often crumble to dust when exposed to air and moisture. Any traces of human remains are treated with supreme care, respect, and dignity.

Egypt Is the Nile

After he recovered from the shock of seeing his homeland through the eyes of the soaring falcon god Horus, an ancient Egyptian viewing a satellite photograph of northeastern Africa would quickly recognize *kemet*. He would see *iteru*, the river, and along it the narrow band of lush green vegetation. He would also see *deshret*, the sandy, lifeless desert that the waters of the inundation never reached. And there would be the same steep, rocky cliffs that bounded his world. High on the western desert plateau, the ancient Egyptian would probably recognize the string of oases, stretched like widely-spaced green beads against the gold-red desert sands.

Although the national boundaries of the modern Arab Republic of Egypt encompass many thousands of square miles of *deshret*, to modern Egyptians as well as to their ancient ancestors, the narrow Nile gorge, and especially the thin green ribbon bordering the Nile, is "Egypt." Most Egyptians are still crowded into that narrow corridor. Although the Aswan High Dam has opened up many previously uninhabitable areas to cultivation and settlement, Egyptians still vote with their feet, electing to stay close to the river that has given life to their land for so long.

At night, especially when the moon is full, modern Egyptians lucky enough to own horses are fond of riding them deep into *deshret*. Forbidding by day, the desert by night is a magical place: cool, windy, empty, and endless. Although they glory in galloping by the light of the Bastet's eyes, modern Egyptians, like their ancient forebears, always return to their river, their homeland, their *kemet*.

Egypt's rapid population growth has also overwhelmed delivery of basic services: water supply, waste disposal, electricity, and transportation. By the early 1980s, demand for electricity already exceeded supply.

Salvage Archaeology

During the planning of the Aswan High Dam in the 1950s, it occurred to some observant persons that the dam was going to flood more than 300 miles of Nubia, including dozens of important ancient monuments and sites. Many had never been excavated or even documented. Additional sites doubtless awaited discovery. Even more troubling, the dam would drown the Great Temple of Ramesses II at Abu Simbel, the smaller temple Ramesses built for his favorite wife nearby, and the monuments and temples on the island of Philae.

The dam could not wait. UNESCO, a branch of the United Nations, appealed for international help. The two major missions were to move Ramesses's Great Temple and the Philae monuments to higher ground. Many other sites and monuments needed to be excavated, documented, and possibly moved.

The vastness of this task cannot be overestimated. A heroic effort by thousands of archaeologists from all over the world poured their combined talents, creativity, and labor into getting the impossible job done. Ancient forts were excavated and documented with astounding swiftness and thoroughness. Several monuments were moved and rebuilt at an open-air museum near Aswan. Temples and monuments that would have otherwise drowned beneath Lake Nasser were donated by grateful Egypt to countries participating in the rescue effort. Most of these have been rebuilt as parts of museums in Europe and the United States.

Because of the international, science-based, technologically sophisticated, well-planned, and perfectly-executed rescue effort, Ramesses's glorious Abu Simbel temples now stand eternal watch on higher ground near the lake, but safe from its waters. Moving the four 60-foot tall statues of the Pharaoh was a supreme technical challenge. Several plans were considered and discarded. In the end, the huge statues were cut apart, hauled off in pieces, and reassembled at their new home. Ramesses the Great, mighty ruler of the world's first superpower, would have expected nothing less.

No individual, no single nation, could have rescued those monuments. The era when a Howard Carter or a Giovanni Belzoni could go to the Valley of the Kings and just start digging is long gone. Twenty-first century archaeology is a scientific discipline, not a treasure hunt.

With its water table rising and economically vital tourism threatened, Egypt may need to organize another massive program of international cooperation and salvage archaeology to help solve the looming food crisis and to deal with the numerous ecological problems caused by the Aswan High Dam.

Egyptian antiquities authorities face new archaeological crises every day. Each time a highway, parking lot, or office building is built, ancient sites and artifacts emerge. Like the dam, these construction projects cannot wait. Salvage archaeologists rush to excavate and document, with practiced speed and precision. With water tables rising and resources thin, preservation of known sites now takes precedence over new digs. And yet, Egyptologists agree, many "wonderful things" still lie sleeping beneath the sands.

TIME LINE

There is considerable doubt about the absolute dating of events before 664 B.C.E. Dates listed here are from "Three Kingdoms and Thirty-four Dynasties" by Dr. William J. Murnane, in David P. Silverman's book *Ancient Egypt*.

3000 B.C.E.	Menes unites the two kingdoms of Egypt, the Red Land and the White Land.
3000–2625 B.C.E.	Early Dynastic Period
C. 2900 B.C.E.	The great city of Memphis is founded.
2625–2130 B.C.E.	Old Kingdom
C. 2650 B.C.E.	Imhotep builds the Step Pyramid for King Djoser.
C. 2530 B.C.E.	Khufu builds his Great Pyramid at Giza.
2130–1980 B.C.E.	First Intermediate Period
1980–1630 B.C.E.	Middle Kingdom
1630–1539 B.C.E.	Second Intermediate Period
1539–1075 B.C.E.	New Kingdom
1479–1425 B.C.E.	Thutmose III builds the great empire.
1353–1336 B.C.E.	In the Amarna Period, Amenhotep IV (Akhenaten) promotes a short–lived religious revolution.
1279–1213 B.C.E.	Ramesses II ("Ramesses the Great") rules Egypt and a vast empire. His era is the height of Egypt's imperial age.
1075–664 B.C.E.	Third Intermediate Period
664–332 B.C.E.	Late Period
343 B.C.E.	The reign of the last native Egyptian king, Nectanebo II, ends. The next time a native Egyptian will rule Egypt is 1952 C.E.
332 B.C.E.	Alexander the Great enters Egypt and is welcomed as a savior. He and succeeding Macedonian Greeks rule Egypt. The Hellenistic (Greek) Period begins.
305–30 B.C.E.	Ptolemaic Period (Dynasty 32)
30 B.C.E.	Cleopatra VII commits suicide, ending the dynastic era. Egypt becomes a province of the Roman Empire.
394 C.E.	The last hieroglyphic inscription is carved in a temple at Philae.
641	Egypt is conquered by the Arabs, and converts to Islam.

RESOURCES: Books

Aldred, Cyril, Third edition revised and updated by Aidan Dodson. *The Egyptians* (New York: Thames & Hudson Ltd., 1998)

> This classic text, newly revised and updated, describes all aspects of ancient Egypt in a scholarly but very clear and readable style.

Brier, Bob, and Hoyt Hobbs. *Daily Life of the Ancient Egyptians* (Westport, Conn.: Greenwood Press, 1999)

> A vivid portrait of daily life in Egypt from 3000 to 30 B.C.E., reconstructed using hieroglyphic inscriptions and ancient painted scenes.

Clayton, Peter A. *Chronicle of the Pharoahs* (New York: Thames & Hudson Ltd., 1994)

> This reign-by-reign outline of the dynasties and kings of Egypt includes many fascinating biographical details, family information, portraits of all the major kings, and lots of great mummy photos.

David, Rosalie. *Handbook to Life in Ancient Egypt,* Revised edition (New York: Facts On File, 2003)

> A wealth of facts, stories, and data on every aspect of Egyptian life and history. This is the ideal first book to read about ancient Egypt.

Jackson, Kevin and Jonathan Stamp. *Building the Great Pyramid* (Richmond Hill, Ontario: Firefly Books, 2003)

> The authors document an actual recreation, using period tools and materials, of the techniques used in laying out and constructing the Great Pyramid. There are excellent descriptions of mummification and funerary rituals. The authors take readers on a brief tour of the history of Egyptology, and bring them up to date with a clear-headed discussion of 19th-century as well as modern new-age "pyramidologists" (and "pyramidiots").

Macauley, David. *Motel of the Mysteries* (Boston: Houghton Mifflin Company/Walter Lorraine Books, 1979)

> A cautionary (and very funny) look at the dangers of too much over-interpretation of ancient artifacts. Reading Macauley will make you a much better (and more skeptical) Egyptologist.

Macauley, David. *Pyramid* (Boston: Houghton Mifflin/Walter Lorraine Books, 1982)

> You will not find a better introduction to the Great Pyramid. After studying this book, you could probably build one yourself. Marvelous illustrations.

Shaw, Ian. *The Oxford History of Ancient Egypt* (New York: Oxford University Press, 2000)

> This book may have more than the casual reader wants to know about the history of ancient Egypt. It is well-organized and extremely complete. The index is superb.

Silverman, David P., general editor. *Ancient Egypt* (New York: Oxford University Press, 2003)

> Chapters written by experts in various fields of Egyptology cover many aspects of ancient Egyptian life, culture, and philosophy. There is not much information about political history, but unusually good coverage of religion.

Vercoutter, Jean. *The Search for Ancient Egypt* (New York: Harry N. Abrams, Publishers, 1992)

> This handbook is a fascinating tour of the rediscovery of ancient Egypt, and the deciphering of hieroglyphics, in the 19th and early 20th centuries. Excerpts from original source documents and actual reports, drawings, and paintings by early explorers bring the history of Egyptian archaeology, with all its glory, disasters, mistakes, and occasionally horrifying incidents, vividly alive.

RESOURCES: Web Sites

Akhet Egyptology: The Horizon to the Past
www.akhet.co.uk
> This is a great site for basic information for novice Egyptologists, with lots of images. It includes the "clickable mummy."

Ancient Egypt
www.ancientegypt.co.uk
> This well-designed resource comes from The British Museum. It has timelines, explorations, history, geography—and a clever opening animation.

Animal Mummies
www.animalmummies.com
> More mummies: mummified pets, sacred animals, votive offering mummies, and victual mummies (mummified food) in ancient Egypt.

The Egypt Archive
www.egyptarchive.co.uk/
> A fascinating collection of ancient Egyptian images, including photos, maps, engravings from rare books, drawings, and historical documents.

Egyptology Resources
www.newton.cam.ac.uk/egypt/
> This is a superb collection of links to reliable Egyptology resources on the web, put together by Egyptologist Nigel Strudwick.

Guardian's Egypt
www.guardians.net/egypt
> This constantly-updated site includes a "cyber journey to Egypt." Go inside the pyramids. Learn about King Tut. Join an ongoing discussion group.

Hieroglyphics
www.17webplace.com/translit/tranparser.htm
www.iut.univ-paris8.fr/~rosmord/nomhiero.html
> At these sites, you can convert your name, or any text, into hieroglyphics.

Life in Ancient Egypt
www.carnegiemuseums.org/cmnh/exhibits/egypt/
> This is an introduction to The Walton Hall of Ancient Egypt at the Carnegie Museum of Natural History in Pittsburgh, Pennsylvania.

Mark Millmore's Ancient Egypt
www.discoveringegypt.com
> This great general introductory site is a good place to start an exploration of ancient Egypt. Learn about kings and queens, pyramids and temples, even get an ancient Egypt screen saver.

The Plateau
www.guardians.net/hawass/
> The official web site of Dr. Zahi Hawass, Secretary General of the Supreme Council of Antiquities and Director of the Giza Pyramids excavations. This site is authoritative and always up to date.

The Theban Mapping Project
www.thebanmappingproject.com/
> The official site of the Theban Mapping Project (TMP), based at the American University in Cairo. The TMP is an effort to prepare a comprehensive archaeological database of Thebes, site of thousands of important tombs and temples.

The Tomb of Senneferi
www.newton.cam.ac.uk/egypt/tt99/
> This site documents archaeologist Nigel Strudwick's ongoing dig at the tomb of Senneferi (Theban Tomb 99). His "dig diaries" are a fascinating look at the day-to-day work of archaeology.

The Upuaut Project:
A Report by Rudolf Gantenbrink
www.cheops.org
> This web site contains the complete scientific report about the robot probes that first investigated the "air shafts" inside the Great Pyramid of Khufu.

BIBLIOGRAPHY

Aldred, Cyril, *The Egyptians* (Third edition, revised and updated by Aidan Dodson). London: Thames & Hudson Ltd., 1998.

Asimov, Isaac, *The Egyptians*. Boston: Houghton Mifflin Co., 1967.

Breasted, James Henry, *A History of Egypt*. New York: Bantam Books, 1964.

Budge, E. A. Wallace, *Egyptian Tales and Legends: Pagan, Christian and Muslim*. Mineola, New York: Dover Publications, 2002 (originally published in 1931).

Carter, Howard, "The Tomb of Tutankhamen," *National Geographic Adventure Classics*. Washington, D.C.: National Geographic Society, 2003 (originally published by Cassell, London, 1923).

Clayton, Peter A., *Chronicle of the Pharoahs*. London: Thames & Hudson Ltd., 1994.

Collier, Mark and Bill Manley, *How to Read Egyptian Hieroglyphics*. Berkeley and Los Angeles: University of California Press, 1998.

Cottrell, Leonard, *Life Under the Pharaohs*. London: Pan Books, Ltd., 1955.

David, Rosalie, *Handbook to Life in Ancient Egypt*. New York: Facts On File, 2003.

deCamp, L. Sprague, *The Ancient Engineers*. New York: Ballantine Books, 1974.

Derry, T.K., and Trevor I. Williams, *A Short History of Technology: From the Earliest Times to A.D. 1900*. Mineola, N.Y.: Dover Publications, 1993.

Desroches-Noblecourt, Christiane (introducer), *Egyptian Wall Paintings from Tombs and Temples*. New York: UNESCO-New American Library, 1962.

Hawass, Zahi, *Silent Images: Women in Pharaonic Egypt*. New York: Harry N. Abrams Publishers, 2000.

Herodotus, *The Histories*. New York: Penguin Classics, 1972.

Jackson, Kevin and Jonathan Stamp, *Building the Great Pyramid*. Toronto, Canada: Firefly Books, Ltd., 2003.

James, T.G.H., *An Introduction to Ancient Egypt*. New York: Harper & Row, 1979.

Macauley, David, *Motel of the Mysteries*. Boston: Houghton Mifflin/Walter Lorraine Books, 1979.

——, *Pyramid*. Boston: Houghton Mifflin/Walter Lorraine Books, 1982.

Malek, Jaromir, *The Cat in Ancient Egypt*. Philadelphia: University of Pennsylvania Press, 1993.

McEvedy, Colin and Richard Jones, *Atlas of World Population History*. New York: Penguin Books, 1978.

McGeveran, Jr., William A., (Editorial Director), *The World Almanac and Book of Facts 2003*. New York: World Almanac Books, 2003.

Michalowski, Kazimierz, *Art of Ancient Egypt*. New York: Harry N. Abrams Publishers, 1986.

Piccione, Peter A., "Batting the Ball," Home Page of Peter A. Piccione, Ph.D., Egyptologist, Assistant Professor of Comparative Ancient History. URL: http://www.cofc.edu/~piccione/sekerhemat.html. Updated in 2003.

Shaw, Ian, *The Oxford History of Ancient Egypt*. Oxford, England: Oxford University Press, 2000.

Silverman, David P. (general editor) *Ancient Egypt*. New York: Oxford University Press, 2003.

Tyldesley, Joyce, *Judgement of the Pharaoh: Crime and Punishment in Ancient Egypt*. London: Phoenix Books, 2000.

——, *Nefertiti: Unlocking the Mystery Surrounding Egypt's Most Famous and Beautiful Queen*. New York: Penguin Books, 1998.

Vercoutter, Jean, *The Search for Ancient Egypt* ("Discoveries" Series). New York: Harry N. Abrams Publishers, 1992.

Verner, Miroslav, *The Pyramids: The Mystery, Culture and Science of Egypt's Greatest Monuments* (translated from German by Steven Rendell). New York: Grove Press, 2001.

White, John Manchip, *Ancient Egypt: Its Culture and History*. Mineola, N.Y.: Dover Publications, 1970.

——, *Everyday Life in Ancient Egypt*. Mineola, N.Y.: Dover Publications, 1991.

INDEX

Page numbers followed by *i* indicate illustrations.

horse and chariot 102
horses 89
Horus 94, 96
Horus lock 86-87
Horus-name 29, 30
Houses of Life 106
hunting/fishing 88
Hyksos 33-35, 73, 91, 102, 108

ideographic symbols 107
Imhotep 23, 69-70
Imperial Egypt 37-50
imperishable stars 103
imports. *See* trade
indestructible stars 103
industry, in modern Egypt 111, 112
infant mortality, modern Egypt 112
inks 71
interior decor 81-82
Inty-shedu 77
inundation 75, 79, 100
iron 108
irrigation 92, 104, 115, 116
isfet 64, 65
Isis 59, 69, 94, 96, 99
Islam 60, 111
iteru 118
Itj-tawy 31, 33

jewelry 41, 88, 88, 108
Juvenal 54

ka 77, 95
Kadesh, battle at 45
Kamose 35
Karnak 43, 45, 55
ka servants 98, 100
Kemet 63
kemet 118
Khafre 26
Khasekhemwy 20
khepesh sword 102
Khepri 96
Khnum 54, 96
Khonsu 51, 96
Khufu 24
Khuit Khufu. *See* Great Pyramid of
Khufu
kings. *See also specific kings*
    depiction of 106
    in Egyptian society 65-67
    and law 101
    mummification of 99
    in Old Kingdom 23
    and sporting events 90
    symbolic dress items of 67
    in Ta-Mehu culture 19
    in Ta-Shomu culture 19-20
    in Third Dynasty 22-23
    and viziers 69

King's Friend 66
kohl 41, 86, 87

labor conscript 75-76
lamps 81
land ownership 68
language 104-106, 112
lapis lazuli 22, 38, 88
Late Period 54
latitude 58
Lebanon 22
Library at Alexandria 58-59
Libya 28, 46, 47, 52-53
licorice 85
life expectancy 83, 112
lighting 81
limestone 25
linen 108-109
literacy 71, 112
loom, vertical 108
Lordship of the Secret of the Royal
    House 66
lotus 20
Lower Egypt 52, 54, 69, 70
low Nile. *See* drought
lunar calendar 105
Luxor 43, 54

Ma'at (goddess) 95, 97
ma'at (principle of balance) 64
    and balance-beam scale 65
    and god-king 65-66
    and law 101
    and nobility 68
    and Osiris legend 94
    and ritual 93
    and *seker-hemat* 91
Macedonian Greeks 57
magic 26, 93-95, 104
makeup 41, 87
mapmaking 58
marriage 20, 37, 67, 82-83
marshmallows 85
mastaba 24
mathematics 22, 102-103
Mazaeus 57
medicine 60, 103-104
Medjay 77
Meggido 40
mehen 90
Meketre 34
Memnon, colossi of 43
Memphis 21-22, 29, 53, 54, 57
Menkaure 26
Mentuhotep II 29-30
Mentuhotep III 30
Mentuhotep IV 31
mercenaries 54, 73, 101
merkhet 30
Merneptah 46

Merykare 113
Mesopotamia 20, 46
middle class 64, 70-74
Middle Kingdom 29-33, 105
military 35, 72-73
Min 97
Mittani Empire 40, 43
Miwer 109
Mnevis bull 54
modern Egypt 111-119, 114*m*
months 105
Montu 54, 97
mortuary temple 43
mud, for pottery 108
mud-brick 18, 80-82, 116
multiplication 102
mummies/mummification 98*i*
    animal cults 54
    canopic jars 96
    cats 79
    grooming of mummies 86
    invention of 96
    linen 108
    medicine 60
    Osiris legend 94
    process of 99
    tomb-robbing 113
    Twenty-first Dynasty 52
music 90-91
Muslims 110*i*, 111
Mut 51, 97

Nakhthoreb (Nectanebo II) 57
Nakhtnebef I (Nectanebo I) 57
Naqada culture 19
Narmer 20
Nasser, Lake 116, 119
native rule, end of 56-60
natron 68, 86, 99
Naukratis 55, 57
naval power 54
Necho II 54-55
necropolis 23, 24, 98-99
Nectanebo I 57
Nectanebo II 57
Nefertari 46
Nefertiti 42, 62*i*, 74, 86
Neith 97, 99
Nekhbet 20, 97
Nekhen 19
Nephthys 69, 97, 99
New Kingdom 82, 87, 108
Nile bloom 115-116
Nile Delta 18, 21, 47, 109, 116
Nile river 19, 27, 39, 64, 114,
    115-118
Nile valley, in predynastic times
    17-18
Nineteenth Dynasty 46, 108-109
nobility 68, 98, 106

DATE DUE

NOV 0 7 2005	APR 2 1 2008
MAY 1 4 2007	
OCT 2 0 2008	
FEB 1 0 2011	

GAYLORD   PRINTED IN U.S.A.